COLOR AND SPACE

In Architecture and Interior Design

COMMERCIAL
CORPORATE
DINING
EDUCATIONAL
PUBLIC
RESIDENTIAL
RECREATIONAL

GINGKO PRESS

COLOR AND SPACE
In Architecture and Interior Design

ISBN 978-1-58423-506-4

First Published in the United States of America by
Gingko Press
by arrangement with Sandu Publishing Co., Ltd.
Text edited by Gingko Press

Gingko Press, Inc.
1321 Fifth Street
Berkeley, CA 94710 USA
Tel: (510) 898 1195
Fax: (510) 898 1196
Email: books@gingkopress.com
www.gingkopress.com

Copyright © 2013 by SANDU PUBLISHING

Sponsored by Design 360°
– Concept and Design Magazine

Edited and produced by
Sandu Publishing Co., Ltd.

Book design, concepts & art direction by
Sandu Publishing Co., Ltd.

sandu.publishing@gmail.com
www.sandupublishing.com

Cover project by studio mk27

Printed and bound in China

SHIKIRI
DIVIDING AND CREATING SPACE
THROUGH COLORS

BY EMMANUELLE MOUREAUX

I will never forget my first hour in Tokyo. I was in the express train from the airport to the center of the city, watching the Japanese landscape go past my window. The greens of the rice fields and trees were shining through the rain. Suddenly, my eyes were attracted by a vivid "blue", standing out against the green background. Since such a color does not exist in nature, I thought at first it was a pool, but looking carefully, I discovered this beautiful blue was the color of a roof. This moment of several seconds was unforgettable. An hour later, I got off the express at Ikebukuro Station, a lively area in the center of Tokyo. Walking through the city, I was shocked by the cityscape brimming with colors. Bright colors overlapping and intermingling with each other, buildings with different volumes and layers of electric cables forming the cutout sky... To my eyes that grew up in a town made of stone, the colors appeared beautiful - like a painting. I was in Tokyo for two hours and decided to live here.

Tokyo made me become aware of color, and made me like color.

The emotion I feel when looking at the Tokyo cityscape comes not only from the fact that it is colorful. There is another very important factor: the sensation of "layers" I feel in the city. Tokyo is structured by a multitude of layers: small houses, buildings with different volumes, electric cables, signboards... All these layers overlap in the cityscape, giving a feeling of depth.

Colors, scattered in a multitude of layers, seem to float in the city.

When I started living in Tokyo, I realized that colors were only presented in non-architectural elements like vending machines or signboards, the buildings or the interiors themselves remaining monotonous. There would be no difference for almost of the recent architecture to be photographed in black and white or color. I was very surprised by this gap between the colorful cityscape and the monotonous architecture.

I decided to create spaces with colors, in order to give emotions to people, as I feel when I see the beautiful colors of Tokyo.

In architecture, color is often considered to be a minor element, decided at the end of the design process, like choosing the color of the walls, color of the flooring or of the curtains... The use of color is in general flat, two-dimensional. I think color must play an essential role in architecture: structuring the space itself. I mean a three-dimensional role.

Inspired by the layers of colors in Tokyo, I use colors as three-dimensional elements, like layers, in order to create spaces, not as a finishing touch applied to surfaces.

"Shikiri": Dividing space with colors

"Colors" and "layers" are expressed in a concept I develop in all my projects, the concept of "shikiri", a made-up word literally meaning "to divide space using colors" in English. Composed of two Japanese ideograms, "color" (shiki) and "divide" (kiri), this made-up word has the same pronunciation as the original word "shikiri" meaning partition in Japanese.

"Shikiri" is a colorful partition series, inspired by the Japanese traditional sliding paper screens or wood partitions. When I realized these functional and beautiful screens are fading away nowadays in Japan, I decided to create a new concept of partitions, which would match the present life and spaces, and bring out the essence of the traditional one: flexibility, layers, transparence, and depth.

I have been developing "Shikiri" partitions with different materials through many of my projects — acrylic sliding partitions for the Magic Forest Clinic, Kaleidoscope Exhibition, ARP Hills Hair and Beauty Salon, glass partitions for Be Fine Office, felt ceiling-hung partitions for the bodies fitness studios, shikiri furniture for Nozawa Apartment...

"Shikiri": Creating space with colors

"Shikiri" is a way of using colors not just as finishes applied on surfaces of the materials, but as three-dimensional elements, like layers, structuring and creating the space. Color becomes structure.

The colors, detached from two-dimensional walls or other surfaces, seem to float in the space and structure. In the Sugamo Shinkin Bank Niiza Branch, "squares of colors" floating in the space structure, giving it its form and depth. In the Tokiwadai Branch, "leaves of colors" play the same role. The layers of colors of Shimura Branch structure and compose the building.

I do not apply colors to spaces. By dividing space and creating flexibility using colors, giving depth by overlapping layers of colors, and structuring the space by scattering colors, I create spaces through colors. I use colors as three-dimensional elements, like layers, in order to create spaces, not as a finishing touch applied to surfaces. Color is not only beautiful. Color is structural, and color is powerful.

CONTENTS

DUMON KORTRIJK
WITBLAD

Location: Kortrijk, Belgium
Area: 50 sqm
Photographer: Witblad

Dumon Chocolatier sells handmade chocolates and the company wanted an interior for its new shop that reflected the craftsmanship and passion that the owners have for their products. Dumon already had two shops in the Belgian cities of Bruges and Torhout. This third shop in Kortrijk is situated in the main shopping street and have to fit well in the design environment and image of the city of Kortrijk.

The shop concept by Witblad is based around treating chocolates as jewelry, as the Dumon handmade delicacies are as pleasing to the eye as gemstones. The entire length of the main counter is molded into angular shapes, with facets referring to diamonds. The large gloss-painted triangles differ in shape and size and reflect the light in a multitude of ways. Working their way from one side of the shop to the other, customers can view the confectionery behind a glass partition. Complementing the molded counter are the Rock lamps from Diesel with Foscarini which hang overhead. The entire color scheme of the shop – white, black and green – ties in nicely with the confectionery within; white and dark chocolate with, perhaps, a hint of fresh mint. The interior has been designed as a shop window in order to be inviting to customers and entice passers-by into the store. Two originally separate shops have been combined into one space with a totally open facade which means, from the street, the entire product range can be viewed.

XOCOLATTI
DE-SPEC

Location: New York, USA
Area: 14 sqm
Photographer: Frank Oudeman

De-Spec's concept for the 14 sqm space lies in eliminating the traditional barriers of a storefront and window display. They created an interactive vitrine-like space that seamlessly integrates with the streetscape.

The walls are lined with custom-designed, floor-to-ceiling bronze shelving systems that are based on the multiple variations of the different sizes of the green and brown chocolate boxes. The wall acts as both storage and a display of multiple graphic patterns, bold and iconic. Customers, daily, choose their favorite chocolate boxes and take it out of the wall resulting in multiple patterns at the end of each day making every day unique. This interaction between customer and display provides an animating narrative to the presentation of the store throughout the day with an insightful discovery for the owners as the largest gaps in the wall indicate the favorite flavors of the day. For the materials of the project, De-Spec chose bronze as it has the richer brown color evoking more artisanal and luxury chocolates.

De-Spec invited Exit Creative to collaborate on the brand identity and together, the two firms created the glowing light boxes featuring each product. This layer of information over the neutrality of the grid enables the customer a more clear reading of their options and flavors. De-Spec acted as both designer and builder and was able to put together a very strong team of craftsman to produce and install the new display system and its components using CNC, laser cutting and casting of various metal works throughout the project.

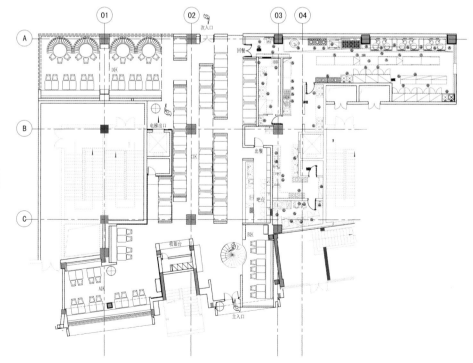

P.S. RESTAURANT
GOLUCCI INTERNATIONAL DESIGN

Location: Beijing, China
Area: 850 sqm
Photographer: Sun Xiangyu

The P.S. Restaurant (Postscript) is one of the hippest restaurants now in Beijing. The customers are mostly younger, and the owner is in his 20s.

The concept for the design was to use continuous, geometric surfaces to create an interesting dining experience for young people. On the first floor, white hallways with mercury looking hanging lights break up the continuous green rectangular strips that dress up the walls and the ceiling. The designer decided to move the green color into glass panels which separate the booths, also making its way to the facade glazing, creating a minty glow ambiance within the space. After ascending a spiral staircase, the second floor has a fresh loungy vibe as the seating changes from booths to individual pod chairs, perfect for socializing and sipping cocktails!

The designer understands the social phenomenon very well and he delivered the idea of "gathering" in this project. It was understood that the target clients would be young working adults, so the design had to be vivid enough to attract young people's taste. Lighting and linear shapes were crucial elements to the restaurant design.

AESOP YOKOHAMA BAY QUARTER
TORAFU ARCHITECTS

Location: Kanagawa, Japan
Area: 23.27 sqm
Photographer: Takumi Ota

Aesop's skincare products emphasize maintenance to restore the skin's natural health, and in a similar way TORAFU ARCHITECTS had chosen a key material that reflects this idea for the store. OSB (Oriented Strand Board) is wooden and has characteristic textures and patterns, which are accentuated by sanding and staining the wood in different ways. Although wood is thought of as a rough material typically used in construction, once stained the wood adopts a stone-like appearance. The result is a distinct materiality which goes throughout the store space.

In order to contrast with the busy surroundings, the existing facade for Aesop Yokohama Bay Quarter was given a simple dark green finish. Immediately upon entering, the walls become light green while white-stained OSB is used throughout, softening the shop interior. Yokohama Bay Quarter is frequented more by families than Shin-Marunouchi, so it was important for designers to create a comfortable space that people can easily enter. In the foreground of the shops are stand-alone functional counters that allow for ease of circulation around the shop. Small stores require an efficient use of space, so the activities essential to the shop's operation have been carefully considered and housed into the "floating" boxes to assist in operational processes. The designers thought about how the volumes of these counters can be opened at various parts when required, and eventually be closed back into a simple box.

CIOCCOLATO
SAVVY STUDIO

Location: Mexico
Area: 32 sqm
Photographer: SAVVY STUDIO

Analysis — CIOCCOLATO is a pastry boutique specialized in custom desserts for special events. In the last couple of years, auteur pastries has grown considerably, which is why brand and product differentiation have become crucial factors for the success of a business.

Conceptualization — The main concept is derived from the already existing CIOCCOLATO, and repositions the brand as a pastry and specialty services provider that caters to all occasions. The Bake & Decor descriptive is used to communicate the new attributes of the company's work towards the rebranding project, without confusing CIOCCOLATO's current customer base.

Identity — SAVVY STUDIO developed a sweet and festive visual identity that uses brightly colored elements and memorable phrases, which go well with any kind of special event.

Actions — Rebranding, visual identity, stationery, packaging, interior design.

OFFICE DUPON
STUDIO RAMIN VISCH

Location: Hoofddorp, the Netherlands
Area: 280 sqm
Photographer: Jeroen Musch

The former villa of the Mayor of Hoofddorp had already been in use as office space for a law firm. The office they left behind were completely reinvented into a modern, spacious office environment that surprises visitors by the contrast between the exterior and the interior.

In order to prepare the villa for its open office function, a partition to provide light and space was created at the entrance for the building. Big open work spaces were created by knocking down as many walls as possible. Light colors were chosen for the walls, floors and office furniture. This not only created space but also formed a neutral basis for the few brightly colored elements that were added. Acoustic panels on the walls were given a bright color, as well as the reception furniture and a sofa in the management office.

The red stairs in the hallway cannot be missed. From the entrance the main meeting room in the back of the office can be seen. A continuing print on the wall and in the staircase enhances the total height and depth of the villa.

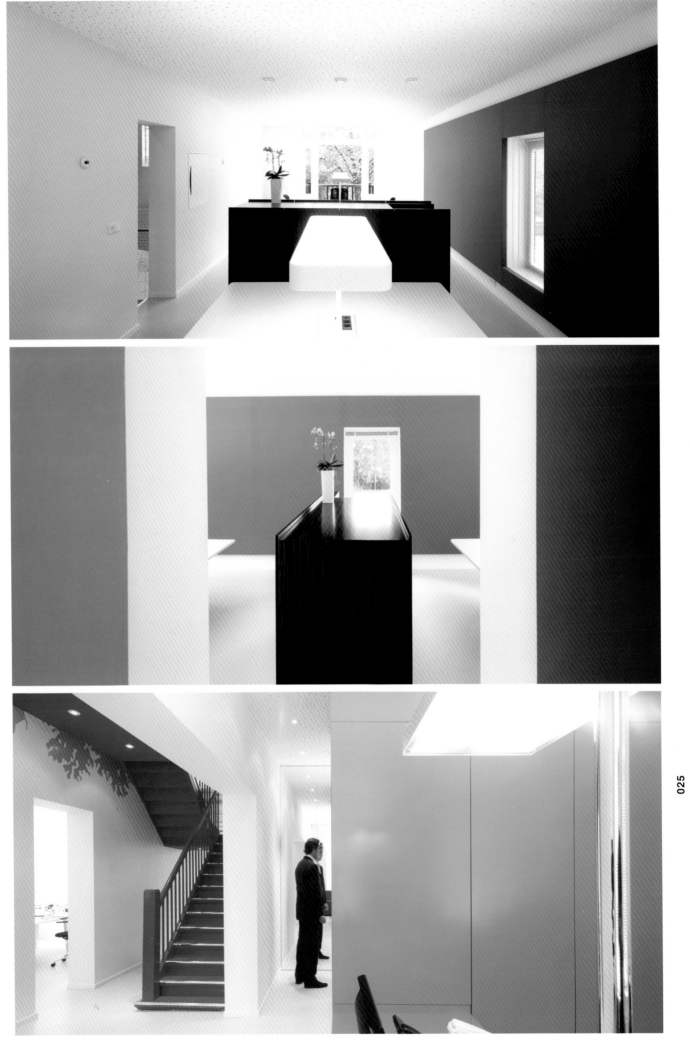

NEODERM GROUP
BEIGE DESIGN LIMITED

Location: Hong Kong, China
Area: 1393.55 sqm
Photographer: Ulso Tsang

Taking 'line' and 'lime' as the representation of dynamics, youth, and energy, the designer created this lifestyle space in line with the concepts of sustainability and continuity. The backdrop for the reception space is a lime colored wall with a front layer of translucent recycled resins panels. The embossed lines on the panel mirror the light beams creating a feeling of movement in the space.

Beams of white dashing lines run throughout the white ceiling and extend to the surrounding space with dynamics. The relaxation zone adjacent to the reception has a consistent lime color tone from the furniture to the carpet. Lines lead the way when the customer is walking into the treatment area. Echoing the linear light pattern in the reception area, in the corridors LED lights also line the walls. Each of the skin care center's rooms is specially designed to be multifunctional, working as a cosmetic room, an entertainment room, and a treatment room all in one. Tables are connected to seating and countertops are connected to hanging cabinets to emphasize the idea of continuity. Everything from curtains, furniture, ceiling patterns, and artwork to tiny details are carefully designed to resonate with the linear theme. The lime colored highlights emphasize the energetic design of the space.

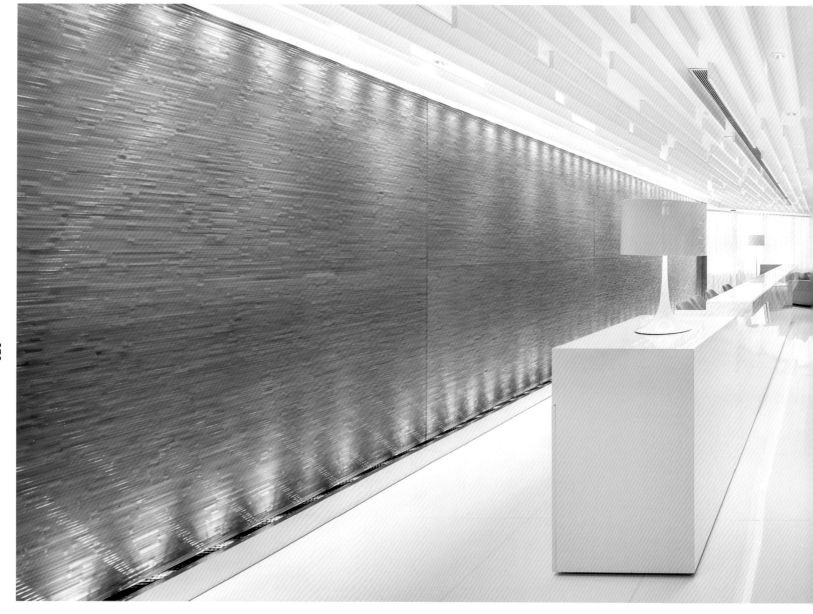

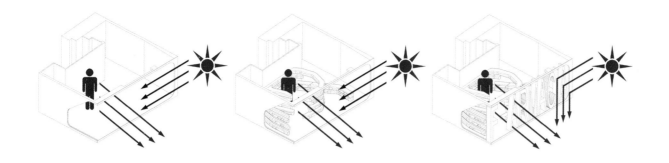

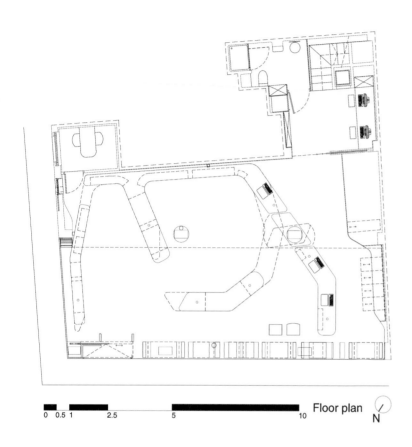

0 0.5 1   2.5   5   10   Floor plan

N

CASANUEVA'S PHARMACY
CLAVEL ARQUITECTOS

Location: Murcia, Spain
Area: 181.18 sqm
Photographer: David Frutos

The entire building seems to lean on a 3rd facade, shaped with the text "FARMACIA", making up a double height shop window. This element marks not only the identity of the drug store, but also provides the necessary solar protection, since the main facade faces west. The sign, which lights up at night, is only understandable from a certain distance - it becomes abstract when viewed from close up.

Inside, behind the sign, a green metallic slat cladding descends from the ceiling through the back wall down to the floor, joining to the same colored epoxy-resin pavement, all together working as a background for the sales furniture: self-illuminated glossy-white tubular elements in five levels, that seem to float and divide the space into different areas. These pieces also make up a rotating desk, a seat, a pulpit and finally provide the necessary space to show the products. The slat cladding hides a small office, an air conditioning system and a glass sliding door leading to a laboratory, toilet, and warehouse mezzanine. The lighting system consists of energy-efficient continuous LED strips on the singular furniture, reinforced by small spotlights where necessary.

Only two colors have been used: "chemist's green" on the floor and the ceiling and "hygiene white" on the furniture.

AZAHAR SCHOOL
JULIO BARRENO ARCHITECT

Location: Prado Del Rey, Spain
Area: 300 sqm
Photographer: Julio Barreno

The architects started by reorganizing existing space: moving the heating room to the central part of the building, creating a definitive entrance in the front schoolyard, and creating a "second corridor" path leading to the entrance.

The main handicap was how this concept could be tangibly experienced by people when the work had finished. That is why the construction decisions became really important. The difficulty of working in the backyard made them plan the design as an assembly construction instead of a traditional brick one. It consists of a steel structure coated with enamelled metal plates for the exterior, and pre-made gypsum sheets for the interiors. These materials are easy to transport and place and they speed up the work at the same time as configuring the construction as a light element with an easy assembly appearance. Rather than being built, the space is assembled.

The exterior is designed in a clear, crisply defined style, while the interior strives to be a pleasant passageway through different experiences. Every meter, something different occurs.

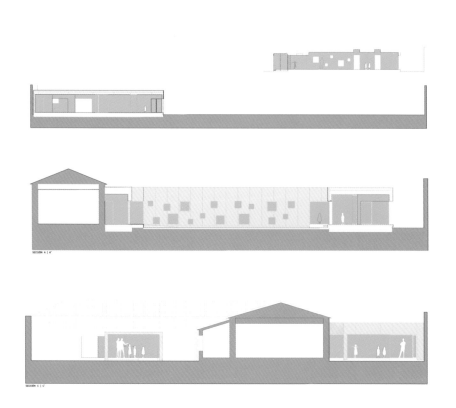

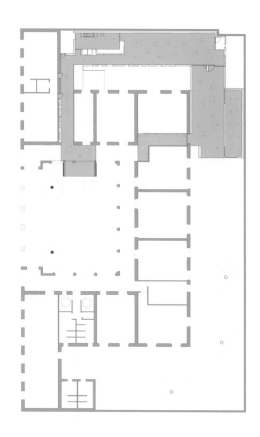

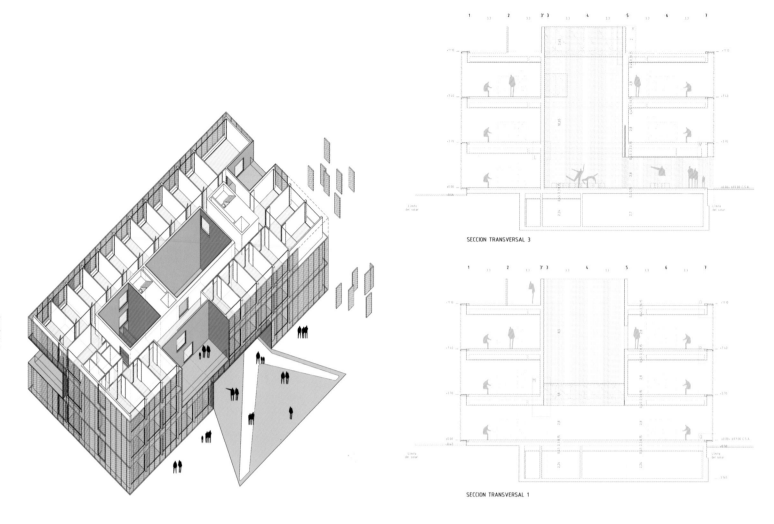

SECCION TRANSVERSAL 3

SECCION TRANSVERSAL 1

SOCIAL SERVICES CENTRE
DOSMASUNO ARQUITECTOS

Location: Madrid, Spain
Area: 2350.44 sqm
Photographer: Miguel de Guzmán

The program for the new municipal social services centre in Móstoles, Madrid, has two strong starting elements. It is a building made up of multiple identical spaces, situated within the weft of a new area of urban expansion, without conditions beyond that of the street and solar orientation. On the other hand, the relationship of the building with the environment is based on a situation of respect for the environment that has little to do with technological systems, but instead values proven logic. Thus, the implementation strictly adheres to conditions regarding set backs from the road and maximum construction volumes. The planned uses were analyzed to optimise routes and to generate a compact building that permits simple maintenance without expense.

The first procedure that was undertaken was lightening the building volume by removing mass to create exterior spaces. Through a process of extraction, these exterior volumes were created to provide multifunctional public or private outside spaces, like outdoor rooms for recreation. The second procedure involved inserting a representative volume that assembled the access and the multifunctional room. Both pieces appear as a unique volume and a continuous, flexible space, permitting colored light to penetrate into the space from the large open volumes. This is the core of the project and its image. The third procedure wrapped the building in a thin regulatory skin that generates a thermal and solar buffer while maintaining internal visual privacy without hindering external views.

CASA CONFETTI
ARCHITECTURAL OFFICE MARLIES ROHMER

Location: Utrecht, the Netherlands
Area: 18,600 sqm
Photographer: Rene de Wit, Akzo Nobel, Daria Scagliola & Stijn Brakkee

The construction of student dwellings in the complex of buildings belonging to Utrecht University has transformed the Uithof site into a full-fledged campus. It will also help to relieve the chronic housing shortage for young people in the city of Utrecht.

Within the line of freestanding buildings ('Objectenstrook') the master plan designed by OMA, the block of 380 independent and clustered rooms presents itself as a solitary mass with a 20 meter cantilever. The spectacular main concrete supporting structure consists of four slabs that together form a theatrical single table leg. The 'leg' and its rocking bench dramatize the main entrance and create an urban rendezvous which distills the encounters and the to-and-from of all those students. The colossal mass which rests on the main supporting structure consists of upright slabs penetrated by longitudinal tunnels, producing a building with high flexibility which will be a long-lasting addition to the Uithof.

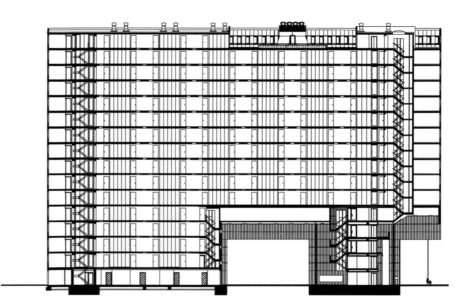

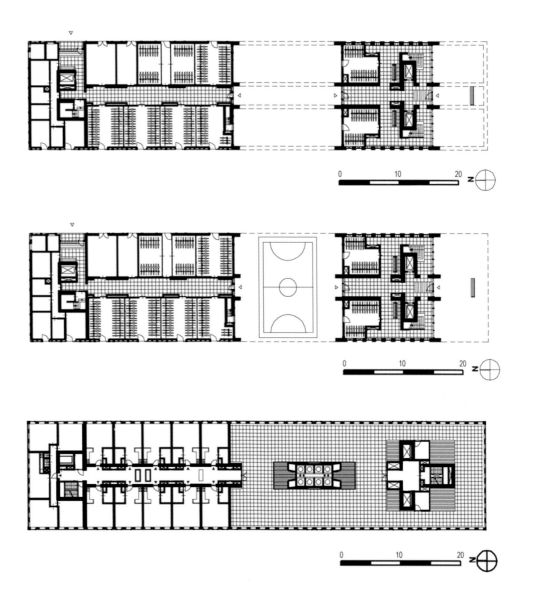

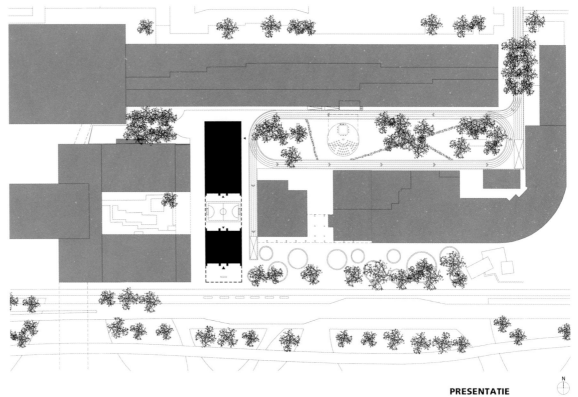

123 SOCIAL HOUSING APARTMENTS IN VALLECAS
SOMOS.ARQUITECTOS

Location: Madrid, Spain
Area: 14,934 sqm
Photographer: SOMOS.ARQUITECTOS

The volume is fixed according to the rigid city-planning rules that prevail within the scope of the PAU de Vallecas and the optimization of the space to obtain the highest number of apartments requested by the developer. Thus, the façade remains as one of the most powerful instruments to manipulate the perceptive scale. The official façade opens towards the commercial street. It gathers the commercial premises and the three accesses (parking in and out and pedestrian). The architects decided to create a single welcome space, big enough to interact with the scale of the building. This hall area is completely open on both sides and its rectangular shape establishes a dialogue with the free-form platforms of the mailbox area.

The building poses reflections dealing with the scale reduction, creating a friendly relation with the surroundings. The façade is split in small colored units that are able to transmit a changing sensation, a dynamic chameleon-like skin. The volume crystallizes through open celled polycarbonate panels fixed over aluminum profiles, creating a sustainable and recyclable skin. Gradations of tones and brightness achieve the right combination in order to make the entire façade vibrate. Instead of the common window roll-up blind, the architects have designed specific shutters for the project. Three-hundred and sixty-nine openings fixed through six different types, made in aluminum and finished with the same open celled polycarbonate panels used in the façade. Energy-efficient, ecological, easy and quick to install, UV-Ray protection and high impact resistance are the main features of this material.

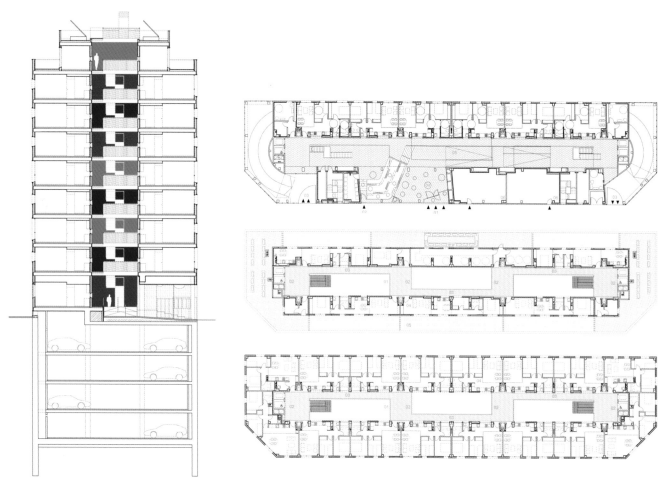

CITÉ DES AFFAIRES IN SAINT-ETIENNE
MANUELLE GAUTRAND ARCHITECTURE

Location: Saint-Etienne, France
Area: 25,000 sqm
Photographer: Philippe Ruault, Vincent Fillon

The idea was to develop a long built "continuum" on the site to interact with adjacent streets. A linear construction that rears up and unfolds but also hugs the ground line to form a low accessible building — one that opens to spacious courts and lifts bold overhangs.

The desire for continuity in construction does not simply reflect the idea of building a legible and unitary urban landmark, it also provides the flexibility that the project needs. In fact, the principle behind this continuum is to imagine a set of "communicating parts" that enable the user-administrations to merge into a whole, one and all, and to evolve according to their needs in harmony with those of other tenants. The absence of breaks in surfaces will ensure that things remain open-ended, with the possibility of extending or reducing space.

The project is like a large "Aztec serpent" rising on the lot. Its body has three identical outer faces, and an underside that is different: a skin of silvery transparent scales and a bright yellow "throat", shiny and opaque.
This dual treatment of surfaces obeys a simple logic shared throughout, which aims at expressing clarity in folds. Depending on these movements, the yellow underside is either a floating canopy or an interior vertical wall, accompanying internal pedestrian movements with its rich luminous presence. The nearness of so much gorgeous yellow brightens up pavements and glazed elevations, casting golden washes over them like sunlight. This is a project that is about bringing together yellow and grey, silver and gold.

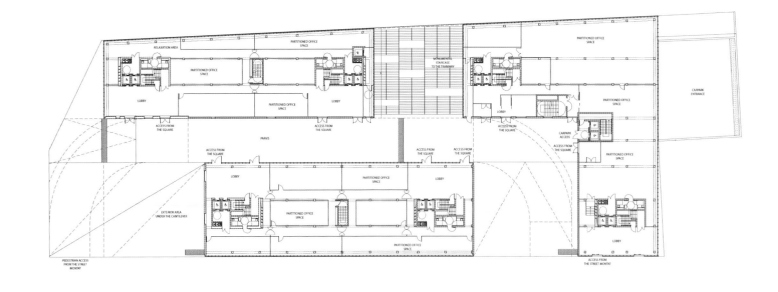

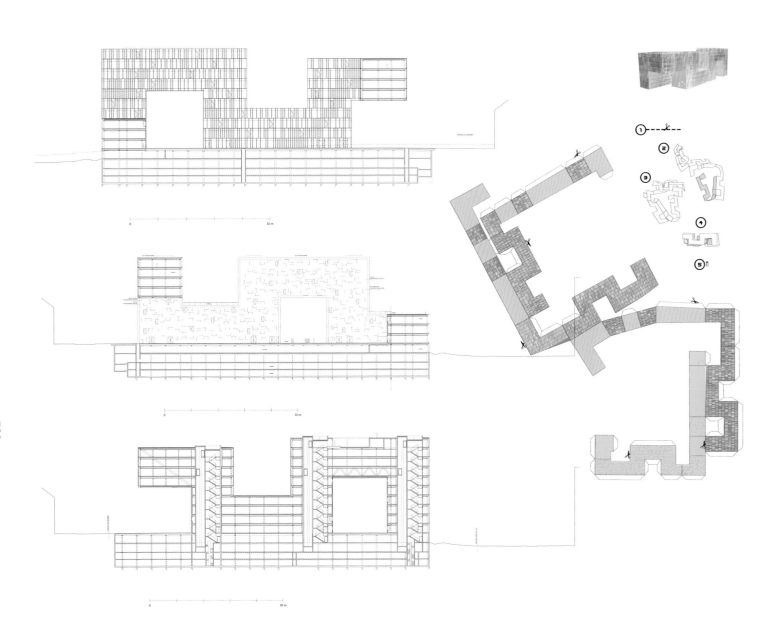

KONZEPP
GEOFF TSUI

Location: Hong Kong, China
Area: 55.74 sqm
Photographer: Zarek Wong, Geoff Tsui

Konzepp, founded by Geoff Tsui and Willie Chan, is a creative project striving to redefine the retail experience. Konzepp achieves this through its carefully curated pieces, as well as the continued development of collaborative projects focusing on lifestyle and quality design products.

Konzepp has three main elements. The Konzepp "space" is a creative retail hub where just about anyone can come in to purchase, browse or learn about the design and concepts behind the brands. Konzepp is a space that can be utilized for work, drinking tea, or discussions over the communal table. It was designed to spark creativity and encourage unique collaborations.

The second space is the Konzepp Lab. This is comprised of a team of creatives specializing in design, branding, marketing, styling, and also entertainment. The team at the Lab coordinates with brands to collaborate and create special release collections, as well as branding and packaging for the range of products, styling for fashion brands, and market events to help launch the new brands and collaborative efforts.

Part three is the "Living Room" project, a retail endeavor appropriately named kouCH, which is presented by Konzepp. At the center of any living room you find a couch where people relax and socialize. This is the main idea that Konzepp is gravitating towards. kouCH gives its patrons a similar offering to Konzepp, only after hours. You can relax and enjoy a bottle of wine, while still being in the presence of creative and inspirational ideas as well as creative minds.

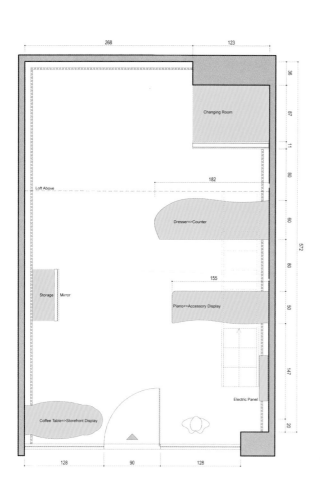

DELICATESSEN 2
Z-A STUDIO

Location: Tel Aviv, Israel
Area: 34 sqm
Photographer: Assaf Pinchuk

The design for the Delicatessen clothing store follows the economical logic of fashion design in an attempt to invert this typical condition. Two main strategies were brought in from the world of fashion and introduced into the space: the use of transient materials and the idea of a disjointed layer that would cover the space.

To begin with, the pegboard material was selected because it is the most basic flexible display infrastructure, which allows for constant change, growth and mutation of the space. Spatial transformations can follow a change in display needs, evolution of the brand or simply the change of seasons. The repeat customer who is used to the change of goods can encounter an immersive transformation and the spatial design can become a commodity consumed on a regular basis.

In addition to the vertical pegboard display, horizontal display fixtures, the counter, the mezzanine and the fitting room were cut out of the pegboard dress and "pulled" off the wall revealing the yellow undergarment. The fixtures are found and recycled furniture pieces (an old coffee table, a dresser and a mini piano) that were chopped off flat where they come out of the wall and painted to match the pegboard. Choosing the material at the beginning of the design process reverses the typical design process where materials are applied onto a concept. In this case the materials dictated the forms and functional possibilities of the elements.

DRI DRI_ST MARTINS LANE
ELIPS DESIGN

Location: London, UK
Area: 45 sqm
Photographer: Carlo Carossio

The Front Room of St Martins Lane hotel is a dynamic retail space. It has housed various creative collaborations with partners including The Convenience Store (fashion boutique), Wallpaper (photography exhibition), Angela Hill (vintage books), The Design Museum (film screening) and Nowness (video installation). This time it will be converted by ELIPS DESIGN into an idyllic Italian beach, complete with traditional decking, colored beach cabins, sun umbrellas, chairs and tables. The customers will be transported to the Mediterranean in the heart of London's bustling centre enjoying their gelato DRI DRI.

The beach cabins are thought of as a way to divide the space and create a back room for storage.

The sun umbrellas are wall stickers that give a sense of perspective to the bidimensional space.

SANTACRUZ PHARMACY
MARKETING-JAZZ

Location: Santa Cruz de Tenerife, Spain
Area: 300 sqm
Photographer: Ikuo Maruyama

SantaCruz Pharmacy, "a healthy world": a 300 sqm Pharmacy organized into categories, where self-service shopping is very easy and pleasant. This is the new brand and pharmacy concept created by MARKETING-JAZZ for the Elsa Acosta Licensed Pharmacy in Santa Cruz de Tenerife.

The pharmacy is divided into areas, according to the products being sold, the desired shopping experience and the brand positioning. Special care has been taken to ensure that customer traffic flows and is spread out through the whole pharmacy. There are waiting areas for the elderly next to the counters, where they can be served without having to get out of their seat, with the SantaCruz Pharmacy staff doing their "health shopping" for them.

Every product is organized into categories and, to facilitate the identification of products, lamps/bags have been designed with the name of the category, thus making it very easy for the customer to shop alone. What a surprise when you stop in front of the counter and discover that the medications are presented on a large periodic table! This immediately inspires a smile, something that definitely makes the shopping experience memorable.

An area specializing in dermo-cosmetics contains a "make-up bar" where technology is used to provide the customer with an analysis of their skin and the most suitable combination of cosmetic products. An impeccable multi-brand presentation using crafted frame moldings and natural stones reinforces the impression of a high-quality product.

PLAY POT
LIM TAE HEE DESIGN STUDIO

Location: Seoul, Korea
Area: 77.62 sqm
Photographer: Youngchae Park

PLAY POT brings the outside world into the interior of the restaurant, creating a space within the space. Taking inspiration from pojangmacha (food carts), an inviting pedestrian friendly space is created inside the restaurant. PLAY POT's sensibility was designed so that the interior space's design echoes the exterior of the building. The use of metaphorical road signs was an ambitious attempt to hint at the sensibility of PLAY POT.

From studying pojangmacha, the material and tarpaulin played a significant role. Tarpaulin is a heavy duty water proof cloth usually made with plastic. It is commonly used by street food vendors in Korea. The material in itself has a slight translucence that allows light to shine through. It creates interesting, warm atmosphere during twilight and nighttime. Pojangmacha has its own merits and own culture. The use of zippers creates windows, allowing the tarpaulin tent rim to be folded up to make an entrance. PLAY POT was a project that stimulates nostalgia and familiarity, and recreates its own culture.

HOSTEL GOLLY±BOSSY
STUDIO UP

Location: Split, Croatia
Area: 1,360 sqm
Photographer: Robert Leš

The "Savo" building, located in the Split city center, was turned into a shopping mall at the beginning of this century and, by a guerrilla action in 2010, was transformed into a hostel in 100 days. Public spaces such as escalators, panoramic elevator and the staircase were kept, and former shopping spaces were partitioned off by a system of walls to create new private spaces within the hostel containing everything necessary – beds, lavatories, showers and toilets. An urban metropolitan character was imbued in the hostel design, with public space created throughout the existing historical membrane.

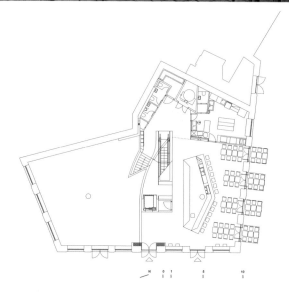

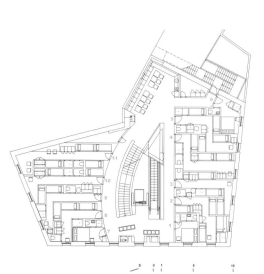

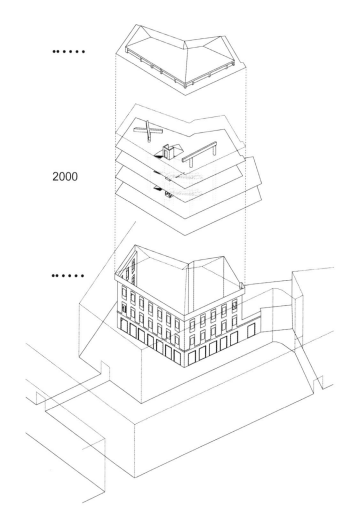

2000

"JOSEPHINE BAKER" GROUP OF SCHOOLS
DOMINIQUE COULON & ASSOCIÉS

Location: La Courneuve, France
Area: 4,500 sqm
Photographer: Eugeni PONS, Olivier NICOLLAS, Delphine GEORGE

In the design of the school, particular attention was paid to passages from one space to another, to thresholds: entering the school, taking off your coat and hanging it up before going through the door into the classroom and sitting down in front of the teacher; laughing as you leave the classroom, and shouting out in the playground at playtime. That is how the building works, from the entrance onwards, in a subtle two-fold movement of advance and retreat. The spatial arrangement recalls the curves and counter-curves of the façade of the St-Charles-aux-Quatre-Fontaines church completed in 1667 by Francesco Borromini. In a protective gesture, the upper floor projects forward to welcome the children, while the glazed ground floor withdraws and digs in to diffuse the drama of separating the child from his or her parents. The corridors change shape and expand in front of the classroom doors. They receive abundant natural light from the zenith, creating tranquil spaces to be used by students for decompression before they take a deep breath and plunge into the work areas. Lastly, the canopy of the playground thrusts out well beyond the ramp that leads up to the rooftop sport areas. This play of compression and expansion, which gives an organic feel to the concrete structure, is further accentuated by use of the color orange. It covers the floors and occasionally spills over onto the walls and ceilings, rendering the slightest ray of sunshine incandescent and lighting up the roof area.

CLASS ROOM   1.01
LIBRARY   1.02
COMPUTER ROOM   1.03
DIRECTION   1.04
TEACHER ROOM   1.05
ACTIVITES ROOM   1.06
OFFICE   1.07
INFIRMARY   1.08
CARETAKER   1.09
DIRECTION   1.10
RESTAURANT   1.11

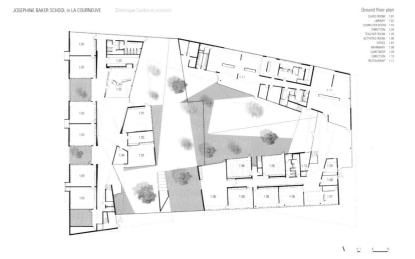

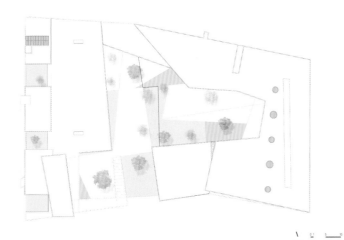

JOSEPHINE BAKER SCHOOL in LA COURNEUVE Dominique Coulon et associés
2nd floor plan
ACADEMY OFFICES 3.01

SCHOOL in LA COURNEUVE Dominique Coulon et associés
1st floor plan

CLASS ROOM   2.01
COURT   2.02
SPORT AREA   2.03
CLASS ROOM   2.04
MULTIMEDIA ROOM   2.05
ACTIVITES ROOM   2.06
DORMITORY   2.07
TEACHER ROOM   2.08

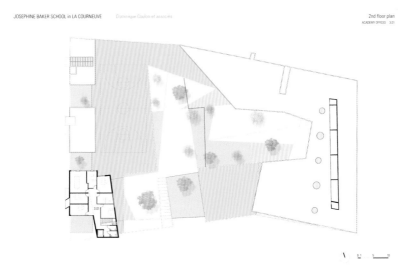

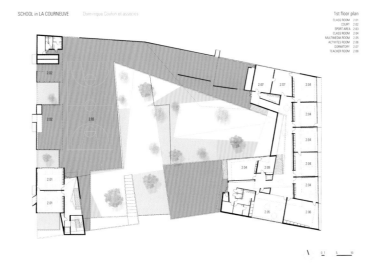

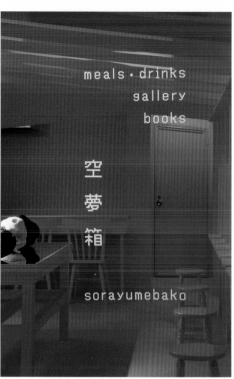

meals • drinks
gallery
books

空夢箱

sorayumebako

SORAYUMEBAKO
KRÄF•TE, YUKIO KIMURA

Location: Osaka, Japan
Area: 42.9 sqm
Photographer: Kiyotoshi Takashima

Sorayumebako is located in the area in which locals live, which is far away from the busy commercial centre. Yukio Kimura designed the shop with the concept of "not blending into the surrounding", following his client's wish to reflect the meaning of "Sorayumebako" in the finished design.

"Sorayume" is a Japanese word meaning "a fabricated dream", that is, a dream constructed during waking life. Having this concept in mind, he designed a space where visitors can feel as if they have stepped into another world, like a dream.

The key color of orange interprets the time between day and night, summer and winter, and yin and yang. It reveals that this is a place for visitors to transition from the yang "daily life" to the yin "private life". He only selected one color in order to enhance visitors' awareness of the shop.

So that visitors can experience a feeling of "bako" (the variant form of "hako") meaning "a box" in English, a series of portal frames line the entrance. He also installed tables, bookshelves, exhibition panels and projector panels in this unique structure, in order to make use of space for many different occasions.

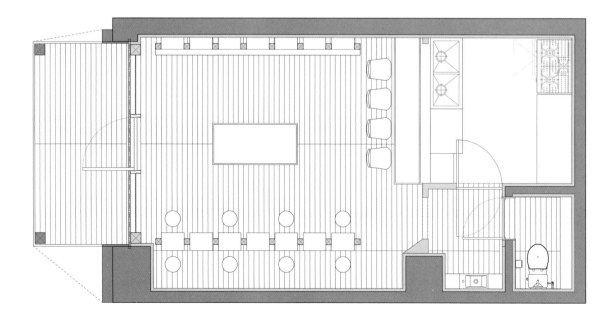

L'AUTRE CANAL
PERIPHERIQUES ARCHITECTES

Location: Nancy, France
Area: 3,105 sqm
Photographer: Luc Boegly

The principle is to "hollow out" this urban space, characterized by its powerful, compact architectural style, and containing the very core of the program (the concert halls, the studios, offices, dressing rooms, etc.), and to pierce through it an interior street in bright red, situated on the ground level to facilitate access for the public and for equipment. This interior street is the user-friendly and functional "Fil Rouge" or "Connecting thread" (literally, "red thread") of the project: it reveals and leads to the entire interiority of the facility.

The Fil Rouge is a multi-purpose, multi-functional area, variable in its geometry and in its ability to host different sorts of events in the reception area, the DJ soundstage-bar and the walkway.

The building is a solid block of concrete, slightly red tinted by the metal shuttering panels used to cast it. The texture of all of the facades is animated by a pattern of cuts in the walls, housing recessed lights that liven up the building differently during the day and at night when it can be turned into a magic lantern in the city, clearly identifying the building as a music center.

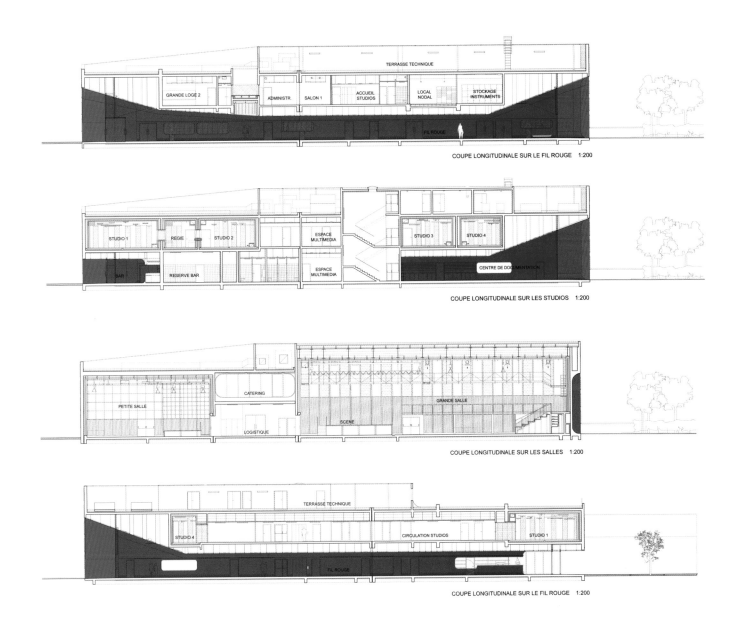

GRANDE LOGE 2   ADMINISTR. SALON 1 ACCUEIL STUDIOS LOCAL NODAL STOCKAGE INSTRUMENTS   TERRASSE TECHNIQUE   FIL ROUGE

COUPE LONGITUDINALE SUR LE FIL ROUGE 1:200

STUDIO 1 REGIE STUDIO 2 ESPACE MULTIMEDIA STUDIO 3 STUDIO 4 BAR RESERVE BAR ESPACE MULTIMEDIA CENTRE DE DOCUMENTATION

COUPE LONGITUDINALE SUR LES STUDIOS 1:200

PETITE SALLE CATERING GRANDE SALLE LOGISTIQUE SCENE

COUPE LONGITUDINALE SUR LES SALLES 1:200

TERRASSE TECHNIQUE STUDIO 4 CIRCULATION STUDIOS STUDIO 1 FIL ROUGE

COUPE LONGITUDINALE SUR LE FIL ROUGE 1:200

FLEX - RED
CEREJEIRA FONTES ARQUITECTOS

Location: Braga, Portugal
Area: 2,900 sqm
Photographer: Santo Eduardo Di Miceli

The building is designed as a undulating perforated block with openings arranged randomly and varying in thickness. Balconies are created by the placement of the cabinets on the building facade. The entrance is accentuated by the formal alignment of the wave front. The garage is conceived as an open space and semi-buried. The corridors are structured as an axis, served by a central vertical access, creating areas of arrival and access to each apartment in the enlarged portions of the corridors. The aim was to use creative building methods in order to obtain a low-cost building that is both aesthetically pleasing and functional.

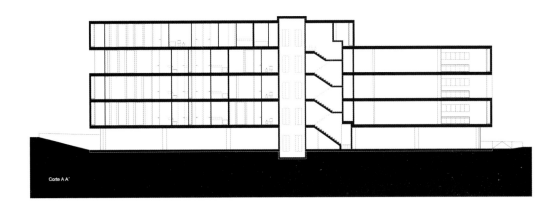

Corte A A´

Alçado Poente

Planta Piso 3

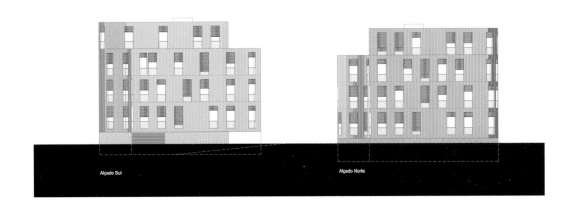

Alçado Sul

Alçado Norte

Alçado Nascente

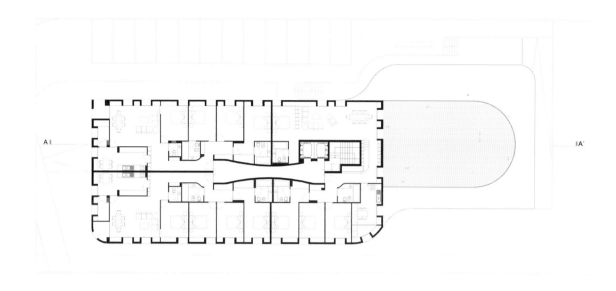

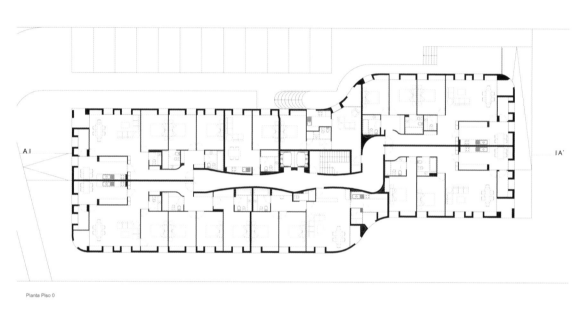

Planta Piso 0

'SHTRIKH-KOD' ('BAR CODE')
MULTIFUNCTIONAL TRADE CENTRE
VITRUVIOUS & SONS

Location: St. Petersburg, Russia
Area: 1,800 sqm
Photographer: Alexey Naroditskiy, Olga Shurupova

The 1,800 sqm site is located in the Nevsky district of St. Petersburg, along house number 5, Narodnaya Street (to the west of house number 5, block A), by the descent from Volodarsky Bridge.

The building has four floors and is rectangular in shape. The main entrance to the building is from Narodnaya Street. Technical, storage and utility rooms are collected in the opposite side of the building. Necessary technical zones are located on the basement and ground floor, and on the roof of the building.

A grocery store is located on the ground floor, while the second floor houses an electrical goods shop. The basement and second floor have small shops selling manufactured goods, located along 'shopping streets'. The shop zones are divided by translucent glass partitions. Evacuation from the building is designed to happen through the landings located at the four corners of the building which have direct exits leading outside.

The figurative facade solutions are a playful reinvention of a product bar code. The facades are composed of alternating vertical slits with glass infilling (window construction with dark grey tinted glass) and bland areas of outer wall. The outer walls are mounted over a metal carcass, with insulation and red metal cladding with grooved vertical joints.

ЮЖНЫЙ (СЕВЕРНЫЙ) ФАСАД

ВОСТОЧНЫЙ (ЗАПАДНЫЙ) ФАСАД

MARITIME MUSEUM ROTTERDAM
STUDIO RAMIN VISCH

Location: Rotterdam, the Netherlands
Area: 1,100 sqm
Photographer: Jeroen Musch

The Maritime Museum in Rotterdam at the Leuvehaven – opened in 1985 and designed by Wim Quist – got a brand new entrance designed by Studio Ramin Visch. The previous grey of the space was replaced by warm orange as the main color. The designers started out with a red carpet – not on the floor, but in steel on the facade and a canopy to the ceiling. This creates a welcoming feel for the outside of the museum and allows for increased recognition of the previously neutral building. The entire ceiling is red, just like the ticket and information counter and a number of walls. Again, the ceilings of steel, like the locker wall, give the space a subtly maritime experience and the feeling of being on a ship. The red floor fits nicely with the grey Belgian limestone and the natural wood furniture. Red ship lights hang above the tables, providing an intimate character and encouraging adults and children to linger. The colors, shapes and materials created an inviting lounge – an important design requirement is met: the Maritime Museum will be a meeting place for the public.

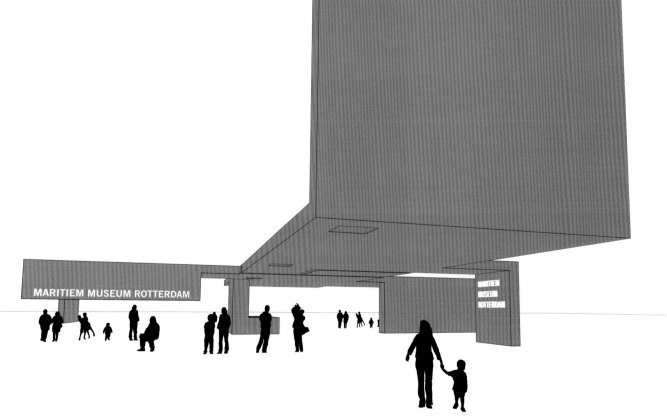

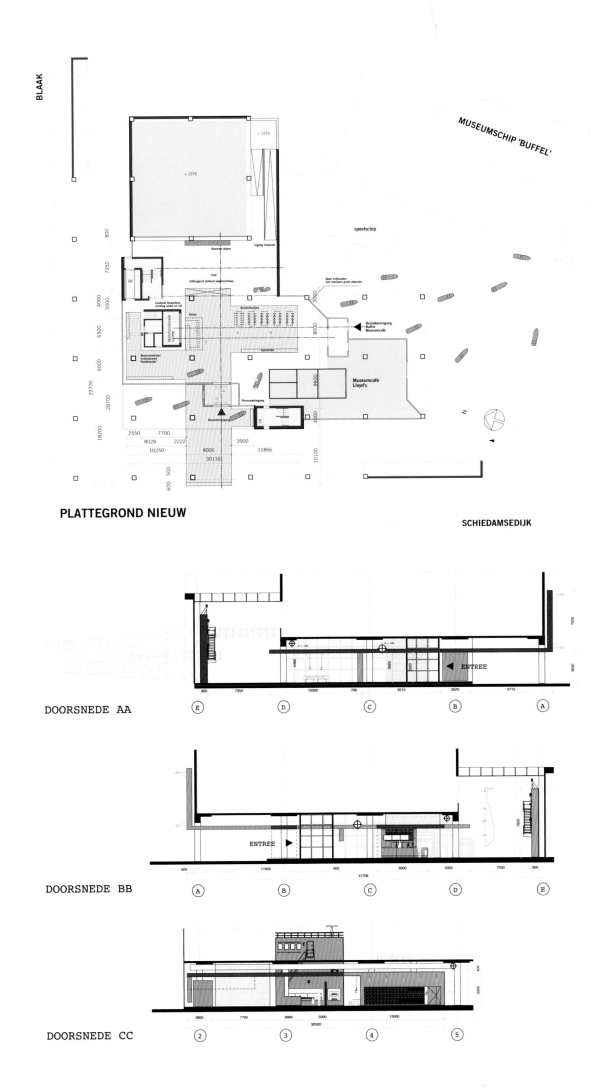

BLAAK

+ 1275

+ 1275

MUSEUMSCHIP 'BUFFEL'

speelschip

Boeient object

Ingang museum

Vide

Lift

Uitkragend plafond wegneembaar

Door schuifwanden tem inhouden grote objecten

Centrale bezoekers, richting toilet en lift

Kassa

Kinderfietjes

Bezoekersingang Buffel Museumcafé

Multifunctionele ruimte

Garderobe

Museumwinkel Scheepvaart Boekhandel

Personeelsingang

Museumcafé Lloyd's

Bezoekersingang

Lift

N

PLATTEGROND NIEUW

SCHIEDAMSEDIJK

DOORSNEDE AA

ENTREE

Ⓔ   Ⓓ   Ⓒ   Ⓑ   Ⓐ

DOORSNEDE BB

ENTREE

Ⓐ   Ⓑ   Ⓒ   Ⓓ   Ⓔ

DOORSNEDE CC

②   ③   ④   ⑤

72DP
CRAIG & KARL

Location: Sydney, Australia
Area: 175 sqm
Photographer: Katherine Lu

72DP is an immersive mural, executed with eye-popping color and occupying the underground car park of an award-winning residence in Sydney's Darling Point by architects Marsh Cashman Koolloos (MCK).

The objective of the project was to breathe new life into the space which, having been rendered in concrete with little inlet of natural light, felt quite dark and heavy. Working closely with the owners, who possess a keen design sensibility, it was decided that the mural would cover all surfaces in a blanket of bright color. There was also a request that the larger wall surfaces be left blank with an eye towards potentially introducing additional, individually commissioned works at a future date. Nevertheless it was vital that the installation feel and function as a complete work in its own right. The resulting design is a dynamic mix of overlapping geometric forms that mirror and respond to the angularity of the architecture. The whole piece is tied together by a winding, ribbon-style device which, acting as a central axis, leads in from the driveway, through the space and out to the garden beyond.

YOUTH CENTER IN RIVAS VACIAMADRID
MI5 ARCHITECTS

Location: Rivas Vaciamadrid, Spain
Area: 1,800 sqm
Photographer: Miguel de Guzmán, Javier de Paz

From the beginning, the project was conceived as the possibility of making the "underground" visible, a construction devised as a radical manifestation of the youthful spirit of Madrid's outskirts, and specifically of Rivas' youth groups.

The project aspires to become an explicit "teen" communication vehicle by appropriating their language and their voices as the ingredients of the project. In this way, the project's team embraces all Rivas's youth groups by means of an open participation process, in which the future users of the centre, combined with technicians and politicians, will contribute their decisions, vtheir concerns, their fantasies and their aesthetics to create a contemporary "social monument".

The end result of this process is a public structure with a punk spirit, intensely burdened with content and articulated around programmatic centres conceived as activity explosions, which are erected as meeting and exchange points for the emerging communities.

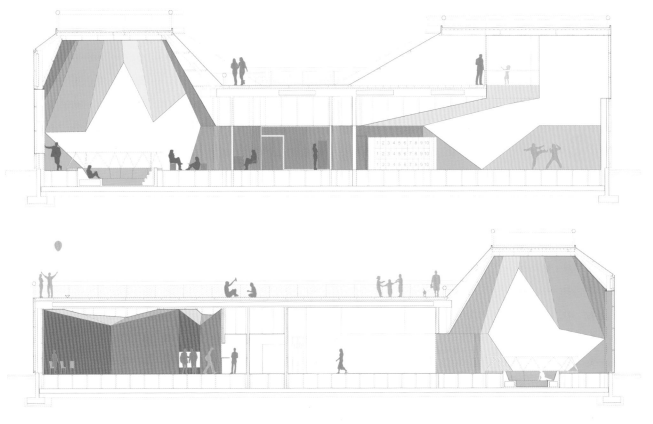

SKYPE OFFICE
PS ARKITEKTUR

Location: Stockholm, Sweden
Area: 1,680 sqm
Photographer: Jason Strong

The project consists of audio and video studios, offices and social areas for 100 employees. The core thought of the Skype software application has generated the design concept for the interior of the new office. Skype is a useful and playful tool that allows chats, voice and video calls over the Internet. From this idea the spaces between the several abstracted interconnected nodes are extruded from the idea of the interconnected world. The scheme of this abstraction replicates itself in the flooring and in the design of the fixed interior. The idea of the loose bubbly furniture evolved from the Skype logo. The Skype cloud logo was literally reinterpreted as a cloud-shaped lighting fixture, shining throughout the chill-out space. The lighting fixture, truly one of its kind, is created out of a cluster of lit up translucent globes of various sizes.

Constructed within a former brewery, a major effort was made in order to accomplish high-end acoustics in the venue, through the use of elements such as specially designed soft wall absorbers which were installed in the space. These efforts were necessary for an office that predominately works with audio and video development. This focus on audio and video development is visible in the interior and expressed in the unique wallpapers with prints of cables, earphones and other devices linked to the audio-video technique.

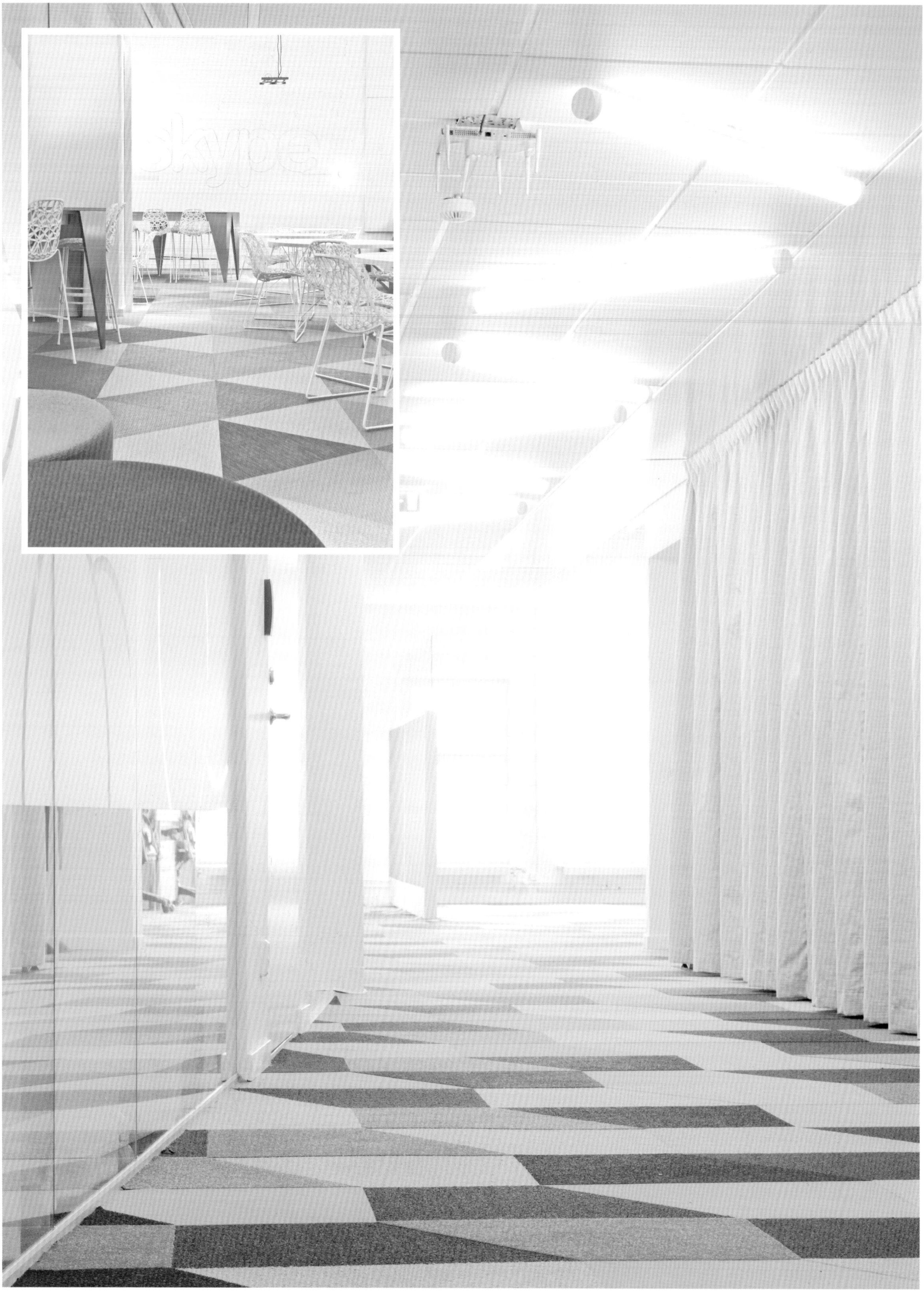

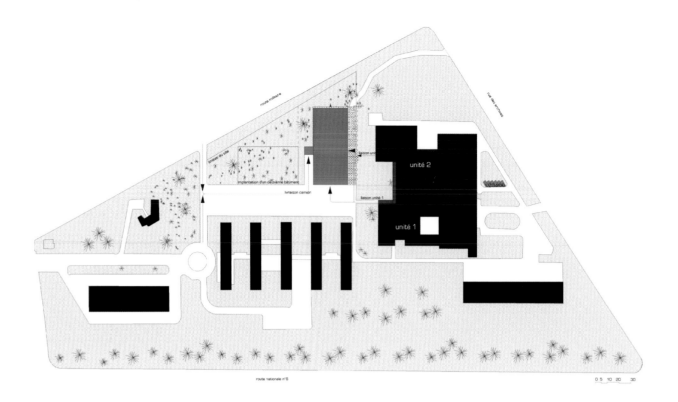

CENTER FOR CONTEMPORARY ARCHIVES
HAMONIC + MASSON

Location: Fontainebleau, France
Area: 5,880 sqm
Photographer: Hervé Abbadie

Located in the forest of Fontainebleau, the site is a combination of undulating terrain, water-sculpted rock formations and gnarled ancient trees.

As one approaches the building, one's impression changes. The skin of the building starts to dissolve and become blurred, folding into the landscape and suggesting a dynamic and cinematic quality. A moiré effect occurs between the overlapping layers of earth colored perforated steel and vibrant green corrugated sheeting, resulting in a surface of constantly changing tones and patterns with incidental reflections of the sky and surroundings. The facade itself consists of a prefabricated concrete structure, insulation, corrugated cladding and perforated steel sheeting, with each layer having its own pattern of openings to allow for ventilation and external lightings. The openings randomly overlap and obscure each other, providing a thickness and complexity to the facade. They suggest that there is an overall pattern but then frustrate the user by never revealing one. Also, their varying sizes do not correspond with traditional human-height openings and hence remove from the façade any apparent scale, making the building even harder to instantly comprehend. What seemed simple from a distance poses more and more questions as one approaches. Finally, this fluidity is reflected internally in a monochromatic world of moving bands of magenta and white. These bands of varying lengths break up the main hallways and mark storage facilities, acting as way-finders and landmarks.

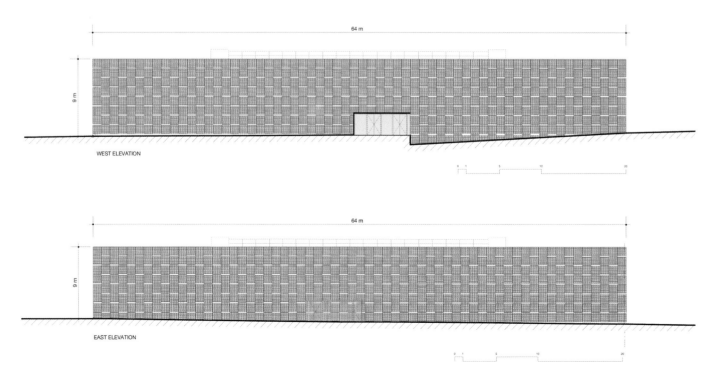

WEST ELEVATION

EAST ELEVATION

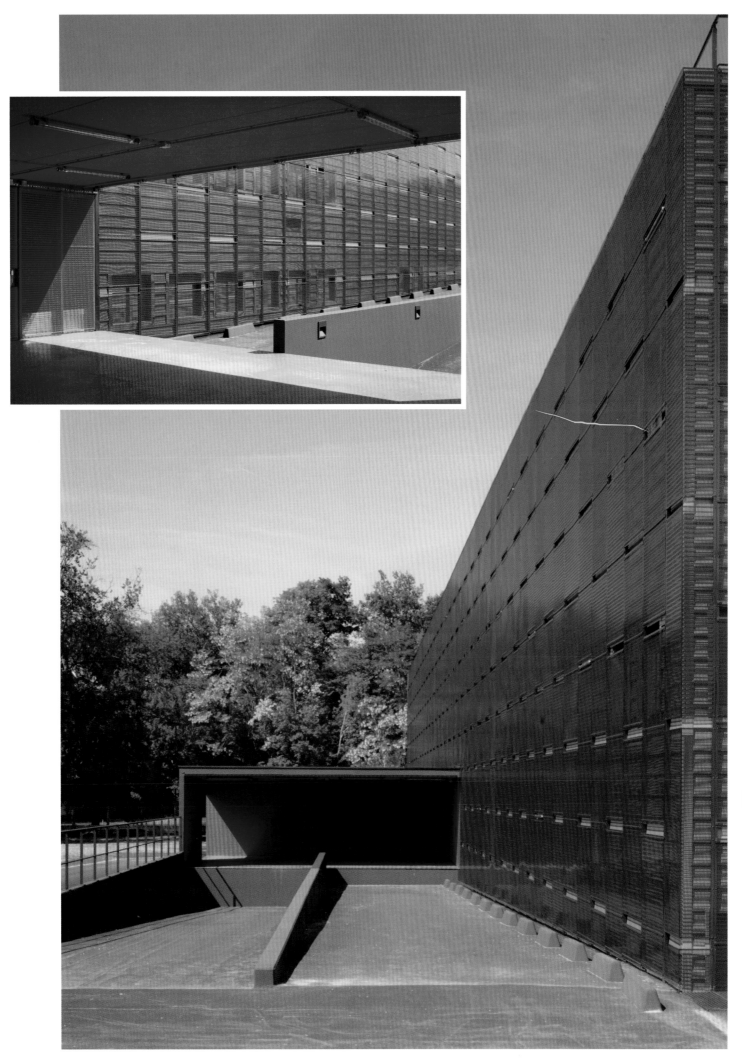

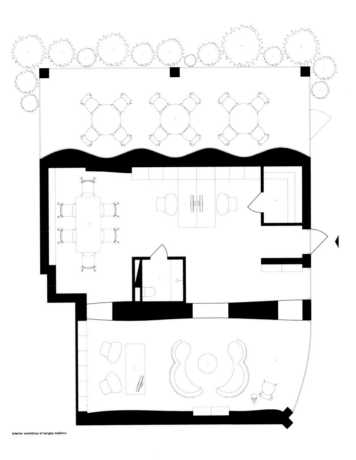

floor plan

1. managers
2. meeting zone
3. designers
4. relax zone
5. products zone
6. wardrobe
7. toilet room
8. terrace

interior workshop of sergey makhno

UKRAINE DESIGN FACTORY, "AZURE"
SERGEY MAKHNO, BUTENKO VASILIY

Location: Kyiv, Ukraine
Area: 126 sqm
Photographer: ---

The office owner wanted the space to reflect the main characteristics of his company that produces design accessories. The office interior communicates a unique design concept to employees and clients. The walls have two coverings: the first one is made with Corian and the second is wooden. The under layer of wood can be seen in the places where the top layer of Corian is intentionally left off. The wood and concrete also both decorate the walls of the bathrooms. The modern office space consists of the meeting space, presentation area, workspace, terrace and storage. In its open space, indirect lighting and bright colors make this work space imaginative and exciting, providing inspiration to its inhabitants.

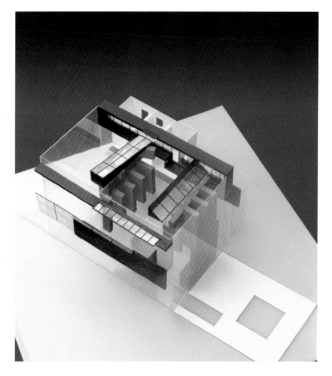

WHITE BLUE BLACK
DAIGO ISHII + FUTURE-SCAPE ARCHITECTS

Location: Tokyo, Japan
Area: 130 sqm
Photographer: Japan Architects, Future-scape Architects

When planning the structure, a single rule was first established. The rule was as follows: the structure of the house was painted in white, the supporting elements in black, and the bookshelves in blue. The supporting elements were bay windows, staircases, handrails, and small eaves for rain and weather conditions.

Blue was chosen as the color that did not conform to the existence of books and erased the gravity of the books.

In each space, the rule decided the finish of the interior automatically without strong relation with the space or function. Through the combination of the three colors, unexpected spaces appeared.

In a typical house, the bookshelves are put in a closed room or on the wall surrounding the room. In this house, the bookshelf space is used as passages for connecting the other spaces. The folding doors divide spaces. If opened, all rooms and bookshelf spaces are joined as one continuous space. When closed, the bookshelf spaces become buffer zones and each room gets independence.

The bookshelf is also a vertical passage for natural light and wind. Through the FRP grating floor, the natural light from the top window reaches the lower floor. On the contrary, the wind passes through the first floor to the highest second floor window, eliminating excess heat and humidity.

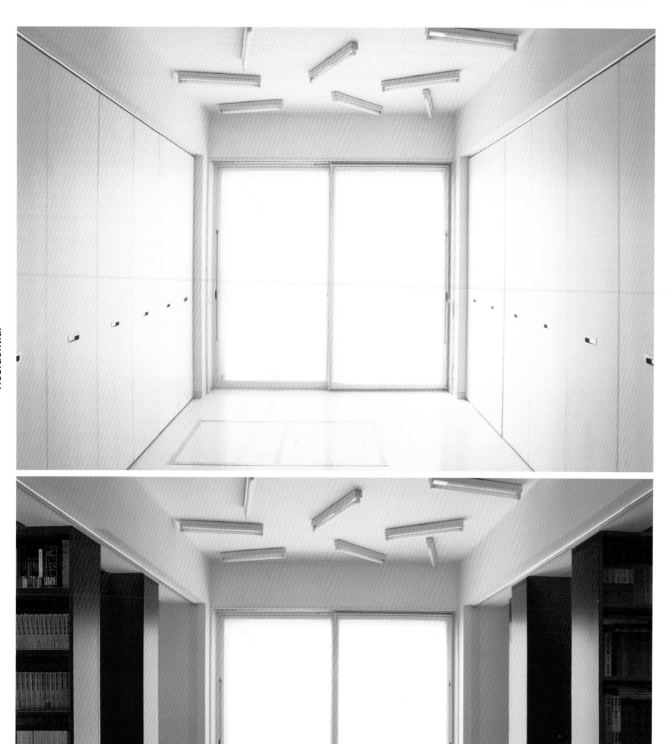

BANSHO-JI TEMPLE
OSSUARY CRYSTAL PALACE
FUJIMURA DESIGN STUDIO

Location: Nagoya, Japan
Area: 91.84 sqm
Photographer: Masato Kawano (Nacása&Partners)

The ossuary entrance has a jintengai canopy with countless crystals hanging down from its entire surface to form an image of a Heavenly River. The glass on the surface of the walls on both sides of the entrance, with stainless steel hanging down, gives the impression that you are breaking through the light above on a Waterfall of Light. You can enter the ossuary's main hall by passing through this Waterfall of Light. From the moment you step foot in the main hall, you will momentarily lose yourself in wonder at the impressive and colorful space that is quite aptly named the Crystal Palace. Each of the 3,000 drawers shaped with 35-millimeter thick pieces of glass in the walls has LEDs installed inside. The light inside these drawers can be controlled with an IC card. The performance of sound and light that seems to have a life of its own soothes the minds of those present. Designed as a place to connect the generations of today with those of tomorrow, you feel not only the beauty, but also a new spatial energy that you have never before experienced. You will be able to think of it as a place where you seem to feel your very own existence rather than form and style. The architects believe that this distinguished ossuary with the latest facilities, the likes of which have never been seen before, will play an important role in society.

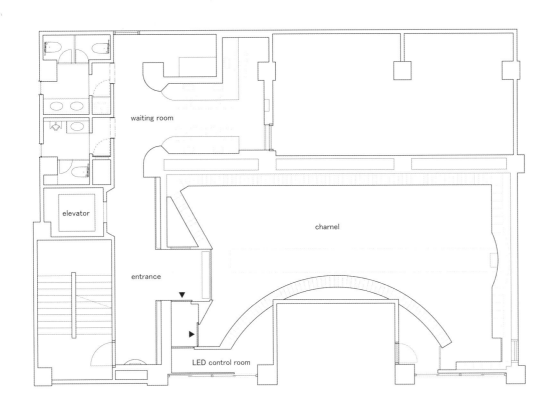

waiting room

elevator

charnel

entrance

LED control room

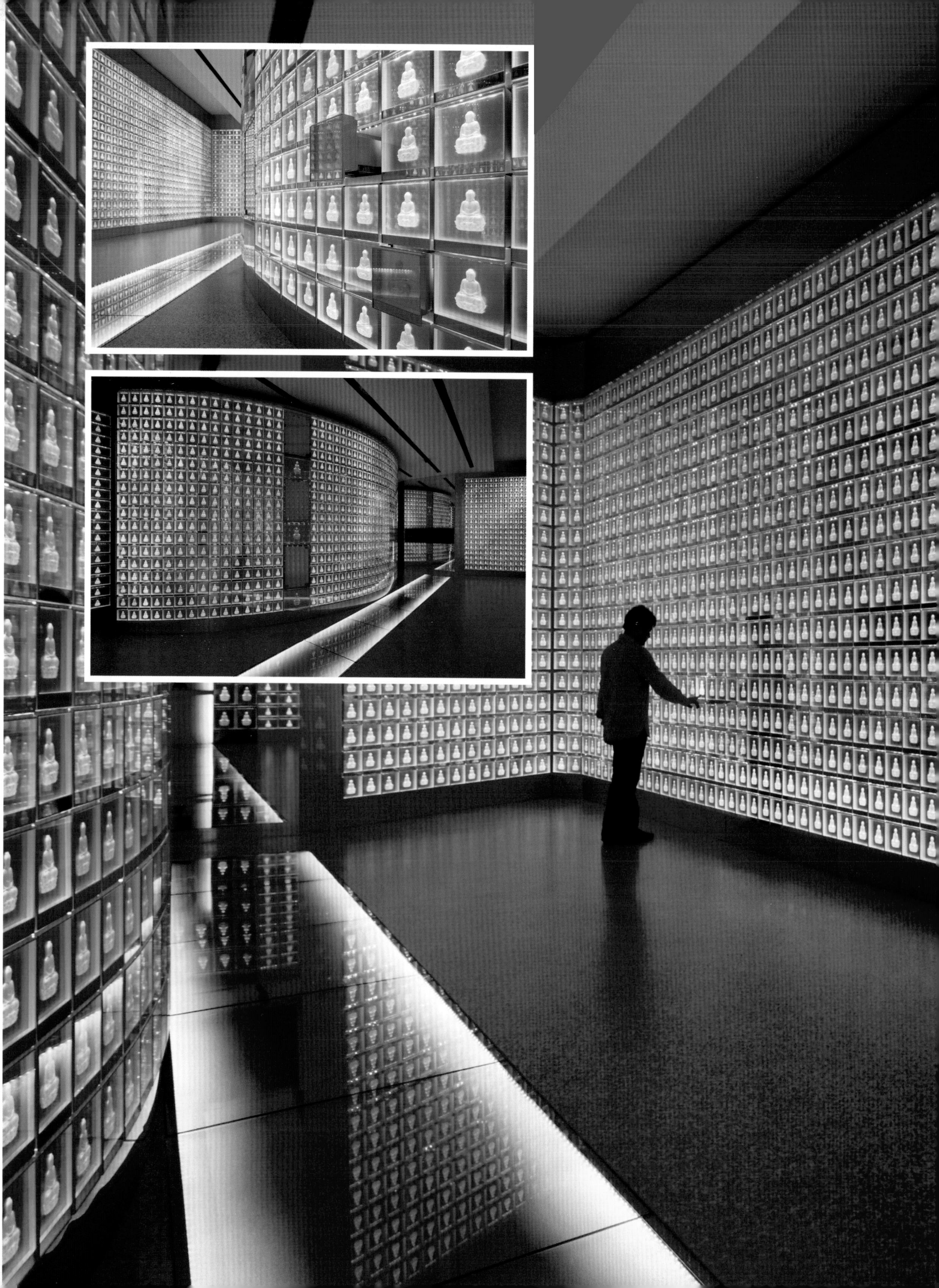

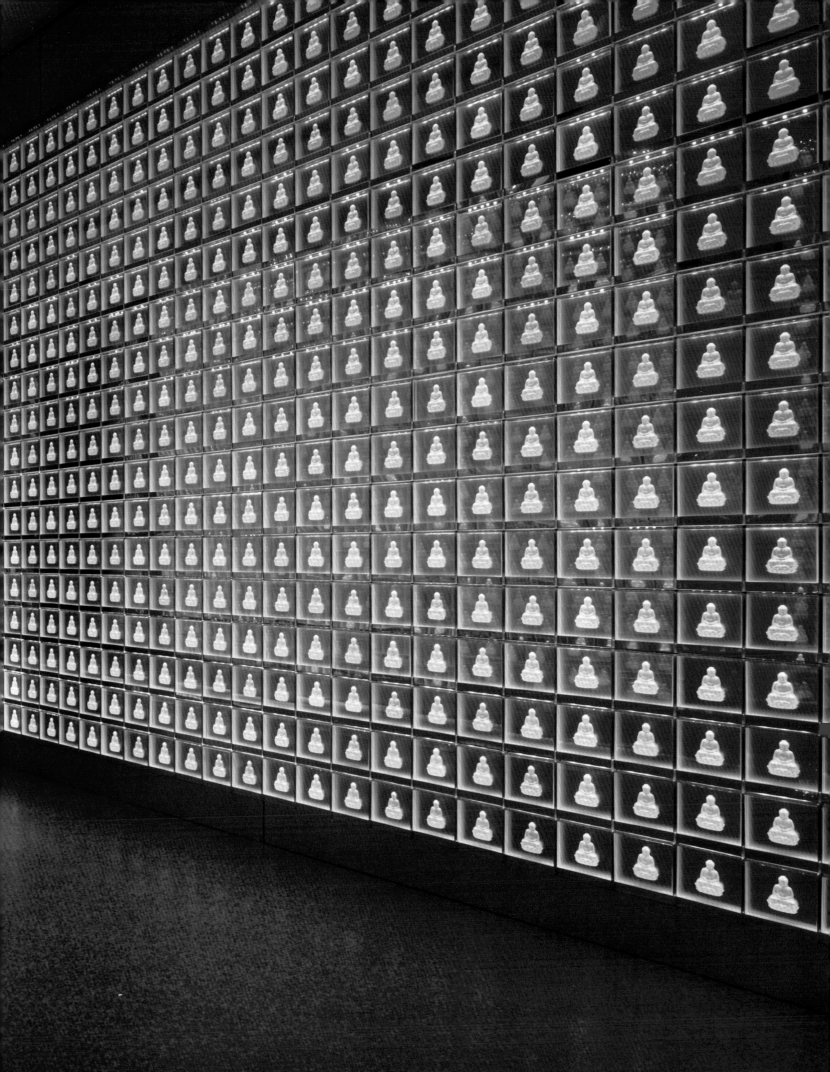

LOFTS YUNGAY II
REARQUITECTURA

Location: Valparaiso, Chile
Area: 1,366 sqm
Photographer: Marcos Mendizabal, Antonio Menéndez

Lofts Yungay II is a collective housing building located in the outskirts of the World Heritage Area of Valparaíso, Chile. This city is one of the largest Chilean ports in the Pacific Ocean. Valparaiso's landscape is very characteristic due to its many hills packed with colorful houses almost falling out of the cliffs. Each house is different from one another, but together they create a harmonic landscape.

The geographical conditions are fundamental design choices. The building is located on a steeply sloping site, and overlooks a ravine. One of the great urban values of Valparaiso was respect for the way the buildings were constructed and adjusted to the geography of hills and ravines. The landscape consists of a series of structures of various sizes and colors, and despite the individuality of each house the result is a harmonious whole. Yungay Lofts II is configured as a series of volumes integrated into the geography of the hill and overlooking the ocean.

RADIAL IN BEIJING
SAKO ARCHITECTS

Location: Beijing, China
Area: 3,100 sqm
Photographer: Misae Hiromatu (RUIJING Photography)

This is an office designed for the advertising company "CIG "in Beijing. The firm was established in 2002, and they already have branches in Shanghai, Chongqing, and Guangzhou with their rapid growth. The clients asked SAKO Architects to design an "office for the advertising company of 2020." The office emphasizes the integration of employees for the sake of encouraging "Communication" and "Collaboration" between them. For the design concept, they used rainbow and the red from the domain color which is CIG's corporate color as the main elements.
The radiating rainbow-like ceiling wraps around the working space, and draws the boundaries between working space and corridor. On the other hand, all employees can get an unobstructed view from their seats. With this visibility, their behavior influences each other, and employees feel a sense of unity.

The plan creates an ease of movement and has many multifunction areas, such as free workspaces near the windows, communication spaces, and resting areas. Moreover, meeting rooms are surrounded by glass walls, and each room has a unique design, such as stairs and train-like shapes. The usage can be determined by people's preferences and purposes.

POSSI ICE CREAM PARLOUR

ANTONIO GARDONI

Location: Brescia, Italy
Area: 220 sqm
Photographer: Ottavio Tomasini

The public space occupies a floor area of around 200 sqm and it's divided into three main areas: a serving and display area (located on the left side under the mezzanine); an entrance and central visitor area (occupied by the long bench, seats and tables); and the mezzanine area (above the display counters).

The whole space is characterized by the very tall ceiling (7m tall) with natural skylight, giving to the main room an airy and clean feeling. On the right wall runs a long wooden bench (15m) made to measure with wood strips and colored cushions of different sizes. The classic bar tables and chairs were redesigned with endless color combinations using plastic wicker to match the adjustable lights fixed on the right wall.

On the left side the ice-cream display and the counters are covered with wood planks in three different colors. These planks can rotate to create different color combinations; above the counters an inclined wall is covered with wood strips with various thicknesses and colors to contain the mezzanine floor and to frame the serving area. A horizontal cut divides this wooden wall to allow a view for the consumers from the mezzanine. The "cut" is defined by a deep stainless steel frame.

The palette of colors (white - blue, beige – brown – light blue, green – red – blue) and the endless thematic associations with stripes (navy t-shirts, fences, benches...) are together creating a vibrant environment full of memory's references without being too literal.

INSTITUTO HEALTH SCIENCES CAREER ACADEMY (IHSCA)
JGMA

Location: Chicago, USA
Area: 9,290.30 sqm
Photographer: JGMA

Chicago based architecture firm JGMA has recently completed work on the first health sciences career academy high school in Illinois. Located in the Pilsen neighborhood of Chicago, this facility represents the emblematic transformation of a neighborhood, a community, and an all-but abandoned building. This 1920s era heavy timber and brick building has been given a brand new color-morphing facade, an addition, and a complete interior renovation. All this, combined with the school's cutting-edge educational strategies and technological teaching tools, have brought this innovative project to the forefront of contemporary educational design.

The existing exterior brick walls have been clad in a new high performance skin, or "rain screen" that has dramatically improved the thermal performance of the building envelope and the overall "health" of the facility. This skin not only has increased the sustainability of the building, but its green and copper, color-shifting facade symbolizes the transformation and progress of a neighborhood and community. This symbolism could not be more in accordance with IPL's mission: "To contribute to the fullest development of Latino immigrants and their families through education, training, and employment that fosters full participation in the changing United States society while preserving cultural identity and dignity."

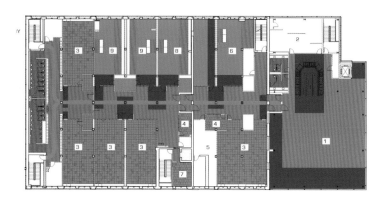

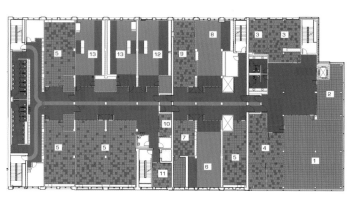

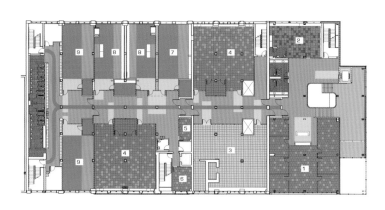

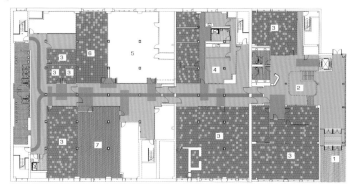

INTERNATIONAL TECHNICAL CHEF COLLEGE UTSUNOMIYA

EMMANUELLE MOUREAUX ARCHITECTURE + DESIGN

Location: Tochigi, Japan
Area: 2162.72 sqm
Photographer: Daisuke Shimokawa / Nacasa & Partners Inc.

TBC Gakuin is the largest group of colleges in the northern Kanto region. This project was a commission to design a new professional cooking school located in Utsunomiya. The concept was to create "spaces for learning that would excite and stimulate the five senses". Symbolic colors and hues associated with particular foods - yellow for pineapples, orange for pumpkins, pink for strawberry shortcake, green for mint, and so on – were extracted from this space for learning about food and cuisine, and incorporated into its design.

Four thematic colors, each in five tones, were used on each floor of the building – yellows for the classrooms and teaching offices on the second floor, pinks for the cake and bread-baking labs on the third floor, greens for the cooking labs on the fourth floor, and blues for the café on the fifth floor. The first floor was turned into a multi-colored space incorporating all the shades used on the second through fifth floors, transforming it into a lively and animated hub where students can go back and forth, as well as gather together. Colorful lobby chairs were placed in the first floor entrance hall, which constitutes the public face of the school. These chairs create a dynamic series of colored lines that seem to flow in a continuous stream from the reception area to the demonstration room. A staggered, stage-like staircase in the demonstration room features a rising section in bright colors, while the walls on either side are painted in contrasting dark shades, creating a generous feeling of breadth that seems to expand outward both vertically and horizontally. Students can choose to sit on any of the 17 differently colored chairs.The gradations of similar hues and square motifs used on the interior walls give students the sensation of strolling through a series of light, nimble rhythms and colors.

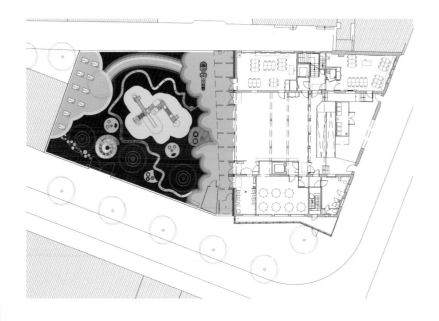

RESTRUCTURATION POUR LA CRÉATION D'UNE ÉCOLE MATERNELLE PAJOL
PALATRE ET LECLERE ARCHITECTES

Location: Paris, France
Area: 1,260 sqm
Photographer: Luc Boegly

The rainbow has become the driving force behind the project, because it both fascinates all children, and is associated with joy and happiness, heralding a time of good weather after the rain. The different colors of the rainbow were used to guide children through the space. They also play the role of identification in the project: the doors of healthcare rooms are red, to mark the urgency. Each level has a specific color. The doors of the classrooms have the same color as their floor. The architects wanted the walls of the classrooms to be white so that the children can fully express themselves. The language of color is used to create spatial familiarity for the children. There are both signs (toilets, differentiation levels, classrooms) and fun (games of hopscotch in the yard, an educational garden, etc). Kindergarteners begin to learn how to write, so the architects incorporated type styles used when teaching the alphabet. Legend has it that at the foot of the rainbow, there is a treasure. The treasure may be the new building, or the children, who are the future. Children's education is fundamental to our society.

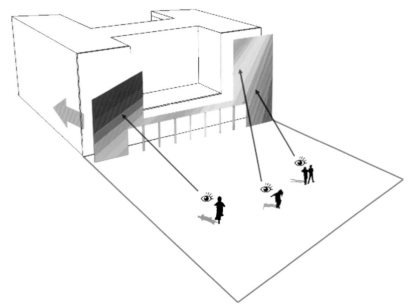

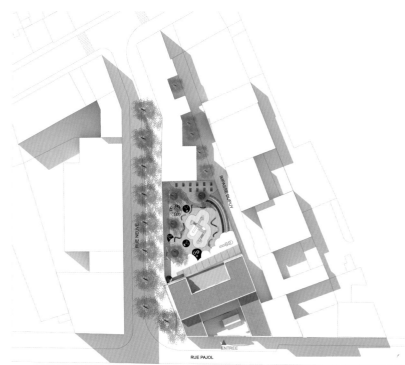

FITZROY HIGH SCHOOL
MCBRIDE CHARLES RYAN

Location: Fitzroy, Australia
Area: 1,300 sqm
Photographer: John Gollings

The model unit of the design is a space for between 40 and 60 students. Following a 'team teaching' approach, the spaces are configured to allow for a flexible distribution of use, accommodating activities ranging from large 'chalk and talk' lecture-style presentations to medium scale seminar groupings to individual private study. This is achieved by a floor plan with an undulating perimeter, allowing optimum supervision to occur within a variety of more discrete spaces. The undulating perimeter is constructed from double brick with a deep cavity, allowing the building's skin to perform structurally, thereby reducing the need for additional framing or bracing. The exposure of the inner skin of brickwork (and the underside of the slabs) maximizes the building's latent thermal stability, considerably reducing the need for additional climate control. The 4m floor-to-floor height required to meet the existing building at each level also increases the quality of daylight deep into the proposed plan.

With its prominent aspect to the street, its dynamic relationship with existing features such as the mature fig tree and its confident, exuberant expression of the aspirations of the school and its community, Fitzroy High School provides a positive example of how, faced with the contingencies of the Department of Education's facilities schedules, architecture can still be designed with a modicum of 'zing'.

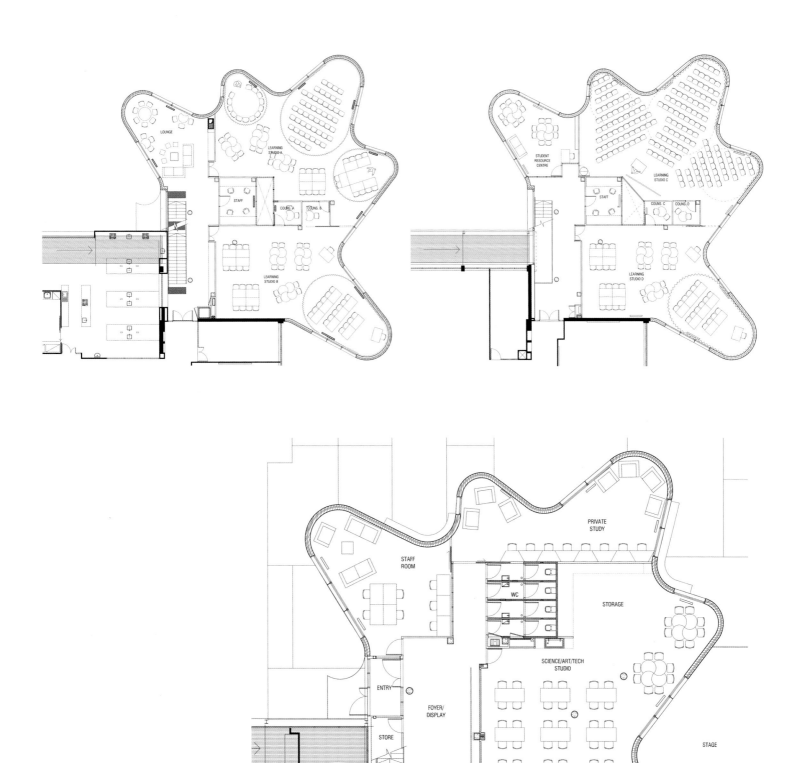

LOUNGE

LEARNING STUDIO A

STAFF

COUNS. A

COUNS. B

LEARNING STUDIO B

STUDENT RESOURCE CENTRE

STAFF

LEARNING STUDIO C

COUNS. C

COUNS. D

LEARNING STUDIO D

PRIVATE STUDY

STAFF ROOM

WC

STORAGE

SCIENCE/ART/TECH STUDIO

ENTRY

FOYER/ DISPLAY

STORE

STAGE

CIRCULATION

RAMP

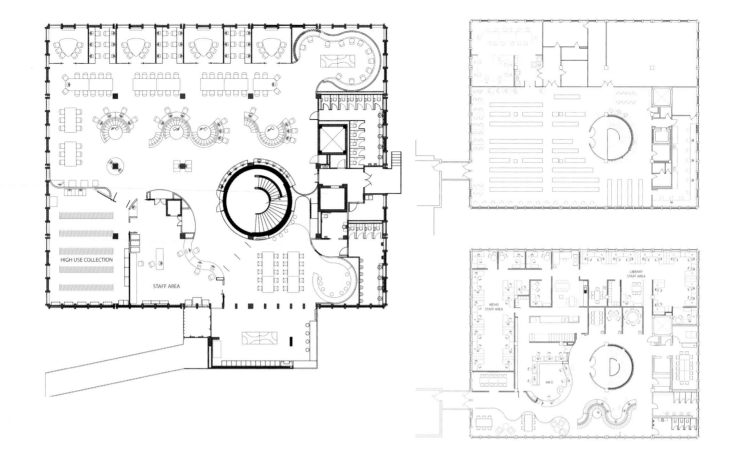

HIGH USE COLLECTION

STAFF AREA

MDHS STAFF AREA

LIBRARY STAFF AREA

INFO

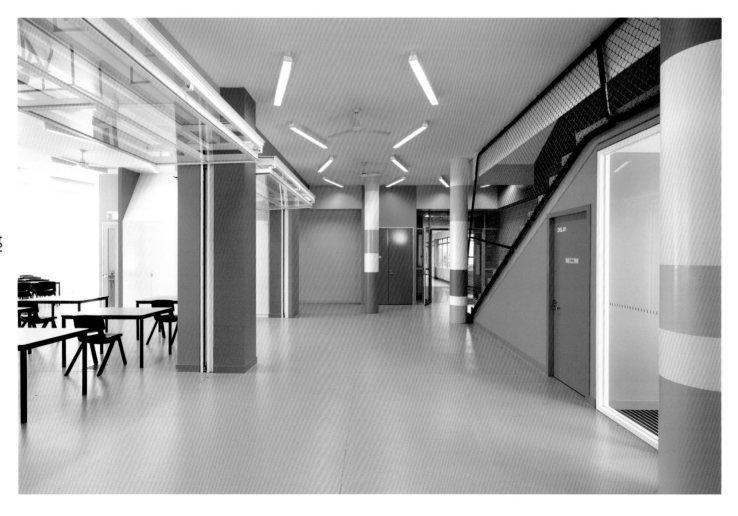

DG.01

PROLOGUE
MINISTRY OF DESIGN

Location: Singapore
Area: 1,550 sqm
Photographer: CI&A Photography

The goal to "question, disturb and redefine" the conventional bookstore experience led to the discovery of some key issues which commonly plague a majority of bookstores. Most significantly, the lack of a clear spatial hierarchy together with the poor visual zoning for distinct book categories sometimes make it confusing to navigate through a bookstore or locate the book you want.

Another issue that baffled the designers was how bland and static most bookstore window displays were, seemingly decades behind fashion retail standards. They aimed to respond to these issues as well as introduce a dynamic public element via a vibrant cafe setting.

They redefined way-finding with a central spine that organizes all the secondary zones and spaces. Curving sinuously through the entire bookstore, the spine begins at the entry window display, continues through the core of the space and culminates at the cafe and sculptural stair leading to the store's second storey stationery section.

To enhance visual distinction, each book zone is crowned by a color coded perforated metal canopy. Experienced as a collective, the eight canopies create a dynamic ceiling scape and clearly guide the user from one zone to another.

The designers have defamiliarized the entry by creating an installation art display starring a Godzilla-inspired creature unpacking books amongst a city-scape of packing boxes which will evolve into a cityscape of books.

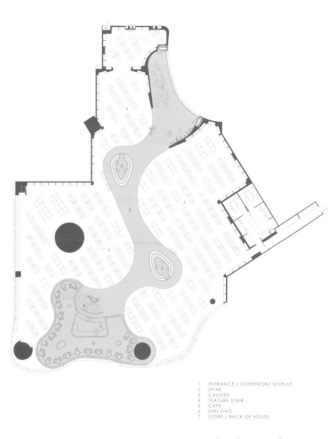

1   ENTRANCE / STOREFRONT DISPLAY
2   SPINE
3   CASHIER
4   FEATURE STAIR
5   CAFE
6   SHELVING
7   STORE / BACK OF HOUSE

PROLOGUE AT ORCHARD ION . LEVEL 4

KOBAN
KLEIN DYTHAM ARCHITECTURE

Location: Kumamoto, Japan
Area: 143.62 sqm
Photographer: Koichi Torimura

Klein Dytham Architects' latest project forms part of the celebrated Kumamoto Artpolis program. This program, designed to provide Kumamoto, a center of the southernmost island of Japan, with world-class public buildings, has resulted in masterpieces by Japanese stars such as Toyo Ito, Kazuyo Sejima, Tadao Ando, and Kazuo Shinohara. KDa's new koban, or neighborhood police station, is located near Kumamoto's new railway station and was required to stand out as a local landmark but present a friendly image. To make the requested sculptural gesture, KDa wrapped the top of the building in a ribbon of perforated steel plate and colored the upper floor volume and the inside of the ribbon with a gentle rainbow gradation. This bold graphic can be seen from all around the neighborhood, but up close creates subtle effects by casting shadows on the surrounding road. While the ribbon was not part of the brief for the building, KDa have cunningly made it functional - a 3m cantilever creates a shelter where patrol cars can park, allowing the police to enter and exit without getting wet!

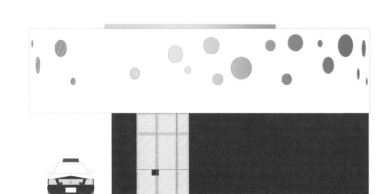

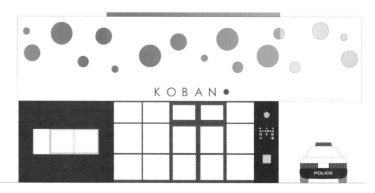

LOUNGE
JEAN DE LESSARD

Location: Québec, Canada
Area: 195 sqm
Photographer: David Giral

With its new project situated in Complexe Ste-Julie, The Lounge, designer Jean de Lessard's firm energizes and clarifies the dim, chaotic space of a bar that has been in existence for more than 20 years. Very economically, the designer successfully weds exuberance and intimacy, clean lines and friendliness.

In order to re-energize a space that previously had minimal personality and was cramped and cold, the senior designer, Jean de Lessard, chose a combination of permeable architectural elements and lively colors in a sixties style. Beside the main entrance, de Lessard composed a corner lounge to serve as a focal point, in an exuberant cubic shape painted with Molinari-style chromatic stripes and opening onto a bowling alley through its glass wall. Customers in the bowling alley can thus see the inside of this architectural "box," enhanced with custom furniture. This furniture, which was easy to build and uses a geometric language, is found throughout the interior of the bar, giving it an attractive visual signature.

Despite numerous constraints, de Lessard and his design firm have created a space that is better structured, more attractive, and encourages better circulation.

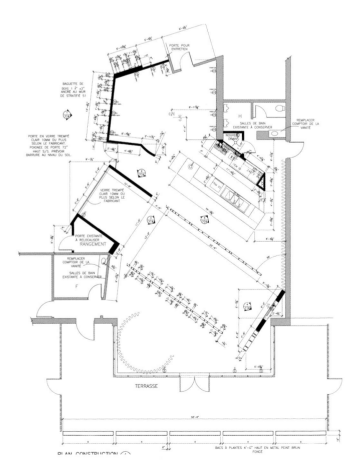

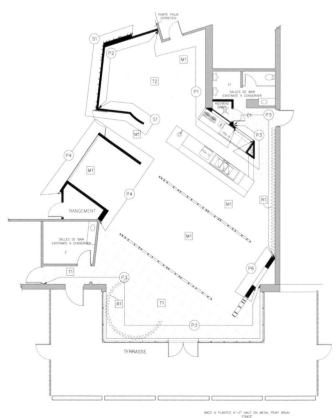

SWEET ALCHEMY
KOIS ASSOCIATED ARCHITECTS

Location: Athens, Greece
Area: 92 sqm
Photographer: George Sfakianakis

The space is characterized by the high degree of transparency which was manipulated in order to diffuse the light and filter the optic penetration. The role of light was highly regarded and thoroughly studied since the beginning of the project in order to create a unique solution for the particular location and user. Light and shadows change throughout the day, giving the space a unique atmosphere every moment. Serenity is followed by tension and drama.

The punctured bronze skin of the main facades creates the impression of the chamber of treasures, of the golden cage which encloses the precious, the rare commodity, the pleasure of the forbidden fruit.

The philosophy behind the choice of materials was in tune with the philosophy of the client. Only raw materials - iron, bronze, copper, and wood - were selected for their natural characteristics and were minimally processed in order to emulate a natural appearance. The purpose was not the stenographic representation of a mystic environment but the formulation of the spirit of the place, the 'genius loci', the atmosphere that will saturate the space and transform it into a true place with its very own distinctive character. The sense of the mythical, mysterious discoveries, and transition spaces to another realm are all the characteristics of the 'Sweet Alchemy' of Mr. Parliaros and those behind the project.

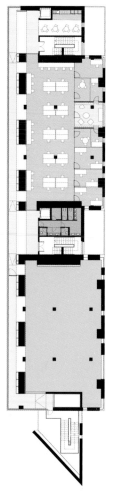
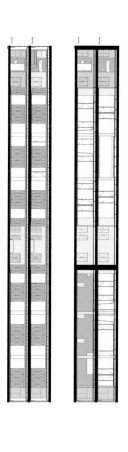

FRAUNHOFER PORTUGAL
PEDRA SILVA ARCHITECTS

Location: Oporto, Portugal
Area: 1,660 sqm
Photographer: João Morgado

The new research facilities occupy two floors in a new UPTEC building in a total of 1,660sqm. Circulation is the project's backbone; all spaces appear along a distribution route located next to the glass façade. This main axis allows access to all different spaces. These spaces, with different functions and sizes, are generated and consolidated through a bold gesture: a waving plane that goes through the open floors, creating different spaces and ambiances.

These spatial and visual dynamics are generated by a free plane that travels through the space and by color, which reinforces the perception of different volumes. The waving surface acts, depending on the context, as ceiling, wall or floor of offices and meeting rooms, guaranteeing visual continuity, movement and flow.

Another important asset to the project is the introduction of several small social and meeting spaces, named silent rooms, which allow for personal retreat, informal meetings, or resting areas. These spaces are intended to generate a highly creative environment promoting comfort and well being among the researchers.

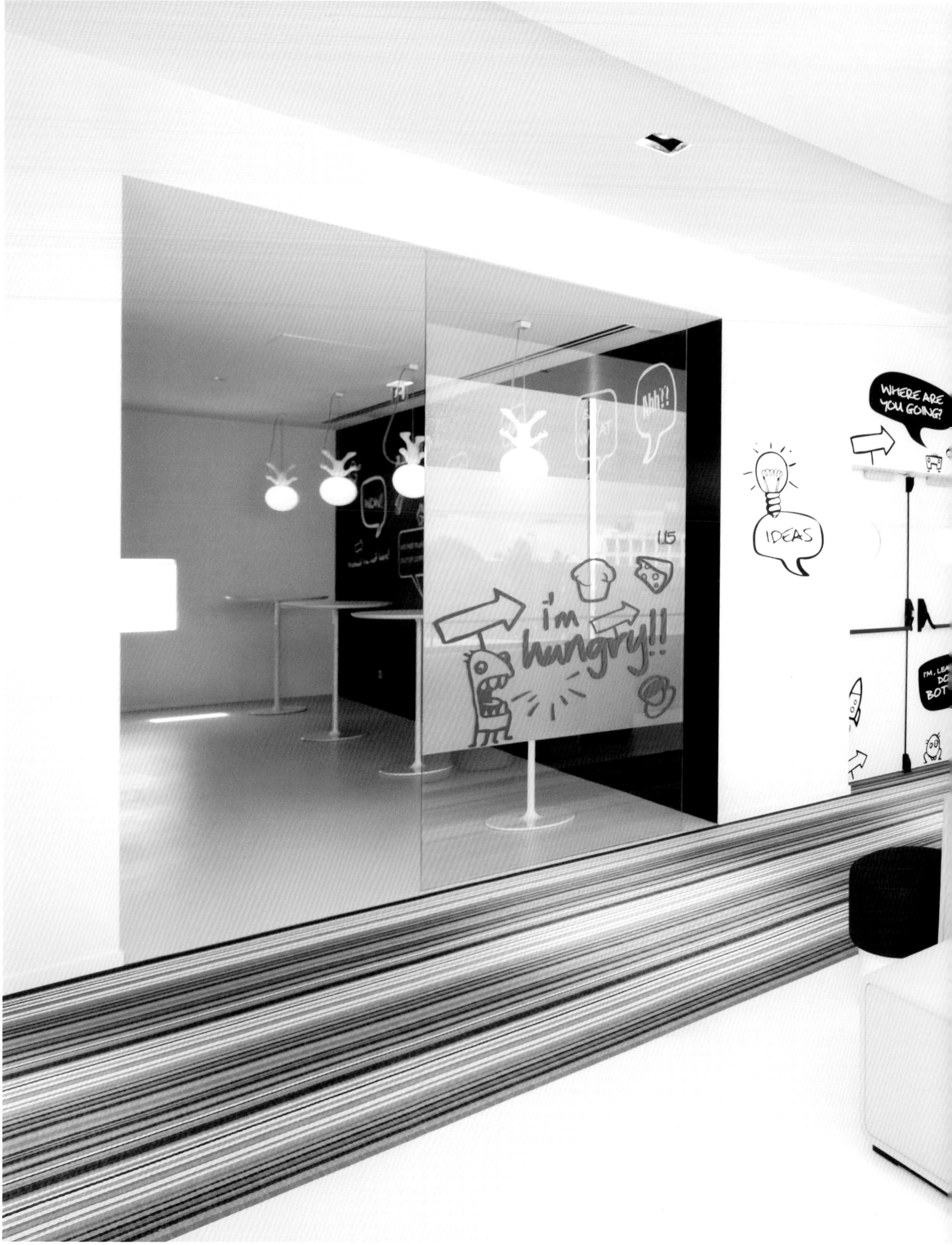
WHERE ARE YOU GOING?
IDEAS
i'm hungry!!

WAX REVOLUTION
ROW STUDIO

Location: Polanco, Mexico
Area: 129.97 sqm
Photographer: Sófocles Hernández

At the entrance of the site a long and narrow corridor was converted into the reception for the salon. After passing the brow bar and turning right down a long corridor, the three main cabins are revealed for the first time. Formed as faceted volumes that expand the visuals of the corridors they are covered with colored mirrors that multiply the views, colors and lights to infinity in a mesmerizing effect. These mirrors are colored with the same tint used to color spheres, but given the fragility of that tint it is covered with a custom made coating that was researched and developed specifically for this project by Sylpyl Industries, giving it the necessary resistance for easy maintenance.

The area of the green and yellow cabins gains noticeable height in comparison to the rest of the site and this sense of height is perceptually continued to the pink cabin, which is located in the lower part, by the continuity of the faceted volumes.

A light bulb in the exterior of each cabin, which is connected to the light in the interior, indicates if they are in use. Inside the cabins all the operational furniture is colored white while the fixed elements are integrated in the same color as the cabins. The floor is covered with natural linoleum to provide the best levels of hygiene and durability.

The colored cabins and their varying geometry guarantee a unique experience for the clientele with each visit to the salon.

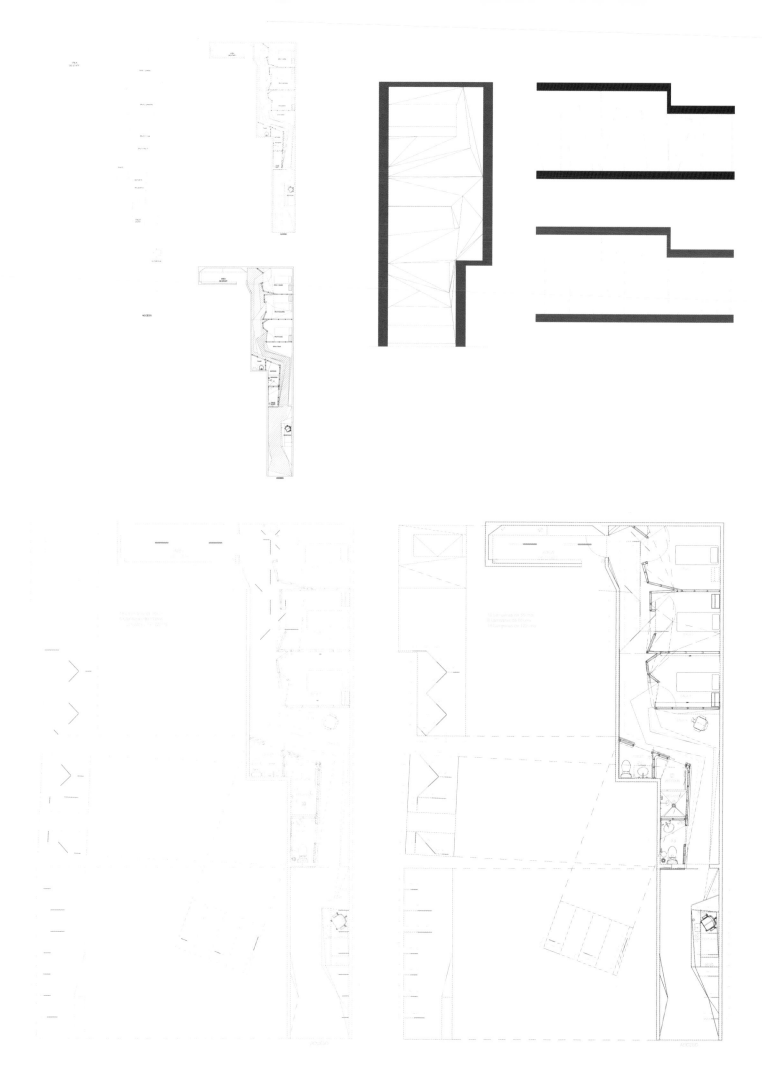

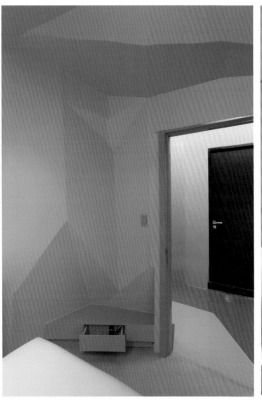

FEDERAL WAY ELEMENTARY SCHOOLS ARCHETYPE-LAKELAND
DLR GROUP

Location: Washington, USA
Area: Each school is between 4,088 sqm and 5,017 sqm
Photographer: Chris J. Roberts

To plan the Archetype on a flexible model, the design team re-examined existing assumptions about educational needs. Initial studies revisited the school's existing program, and found the opportunity to simplify the list of spaces into groupings by type (size, basic function, systems needs). The team then distilled this simplified list into a program of fundamental learning spaces, where each space is defined by capacity and usage patterns. This generic program is a huge change in K-12 design. It supports each school's current, specific program needs but gives them ample ability to adapt to changes over time.

The architectural concept enables adaptation based on site-specific influencing factors, including immediate site topography, surrounding community patterns of use and access, and district-wide relationships. In accordance with the client's goals, the archetype is readily recognizable by its consistent use of an architectural language of lower volumes ("bars") and higher volumes ("lanterns"), and the application of color.

While all spaces engage users through bold color, natural daylight and connections to the outdoors, the geometric formality of the north-south learning spaces contrasts with a playful Network transept. The Network provides a clear connecting pathway (from the western public side of the school to the library/ wetlands on the west) for student and community use of the school. Individual areas for different uses (group learning, gathering, events, play, display, library, lunchroom, etc.) are defined by structural accents and color, but remain largely open to one another, encouraging progression and connection through the school while still providing distinct spaces.

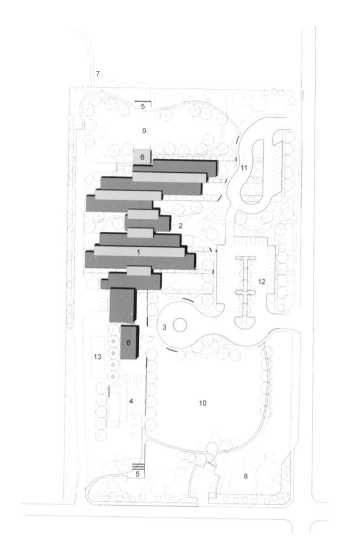

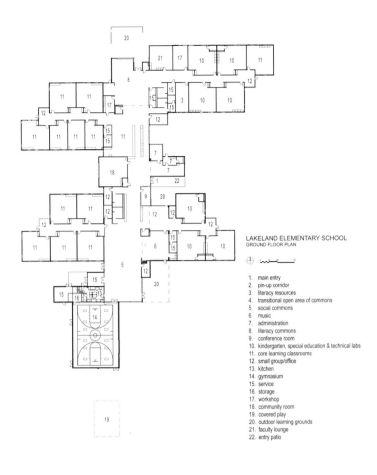

LAKELAND ELEMENTARY SCHOOL
GROUND FLOOR PLAN

1. main entry
2. pin-up corridor
3. literacy resources
4. transitional open area of commons
5. social commons
6. music
7. administration
8. literacy commons
9. conference room
10. kindergarten, special education & technical labs
11. core learning classrooms
12. small group/office
13. kitchen
14. gymnasium
15. service
16. storage
17. workshop
18. community room
19. covered play
20. outdoor learning grounds
21. faculty lounge
22. entry patio

KYMENLAAKSO UAS, WORKSHOP
ARCHITECTS NRT LTD

Location: Kouvola, Finland
Area: 4,050 sqm
Photographer: Tuomas Uusheimo, Mikael Linden

Workshop building is a part of Kymenlaakso UAS campus. The task was to place relatively large workshop spaces at the campus area consisting of old army barracks, without disturbing the hierarchy of the built environment. The building is planned for students studying design and restoration. Workshops are linked to other university learning spaces so that students can first use the classrooms and sketching areas at the old brick barracks and then move on to the workshop spaces to realize their projects. The building was placed partly underground in order to maintain free views to and from the old parade square which is the heart of the campus area. The only part coming up through this "ground level" is a class pavilion containing an exhibition space and a cafe. The pavilion is meant to act as a big showroom where student work can be lifted up to the ceiling and be shown to everyone arriving at the campus area.

Since most of the spaces were placed partly underground, the natural lighting and colors were important considerations for the architects. The class pavilion works as an enormous skylight giving light to the central parts of the building. The only facade south. The wall is made of glass and is covered with spectrum colored metal mesh to protect spaces against overheating. Also almost all dividing walls inside are made of glass. The floors and ceiling are or white colors in order to reflect light as far into the building as possible.

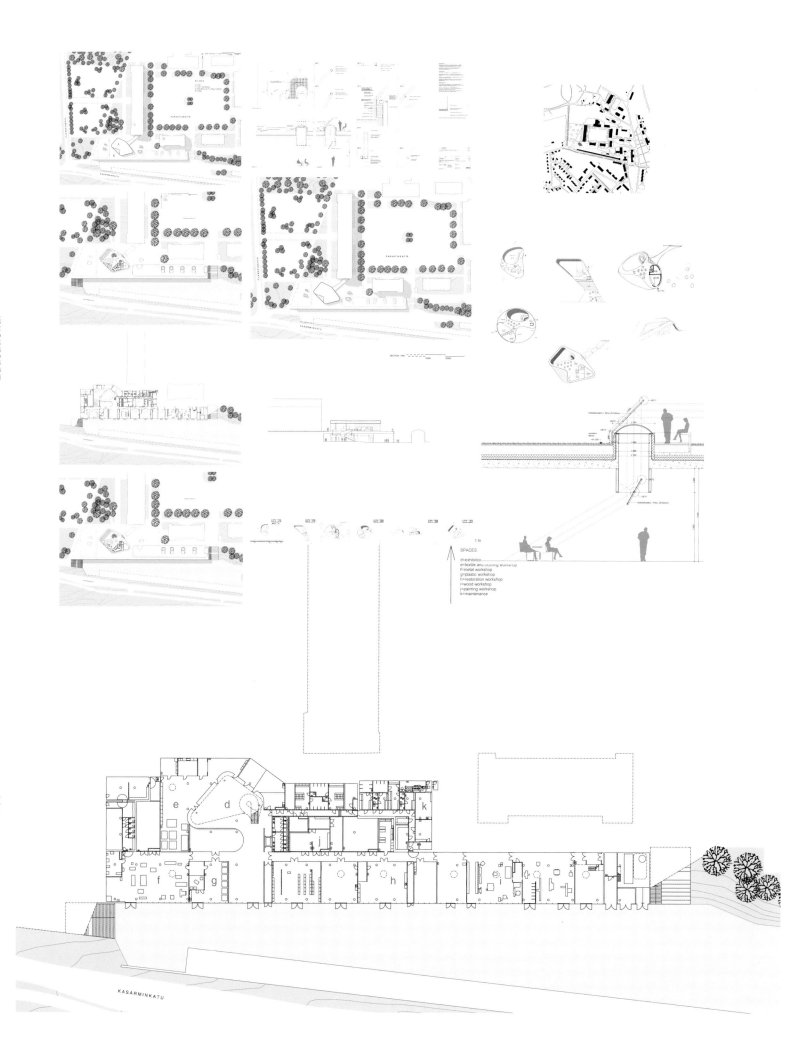

SPACES

d=exhibition
e=textile and clothing workshop
f=metal workshop
g=plastic workshop
h=restoration workshop
i=wood workshop
j=painting workshop
k=maintenance

KASARMINKATU

189

82 STATE SUBSIDIZED HOUSING BUILDING
AMANN-CÁNOVAS-MARURI

Location: Madrid, Spain
Area: 4441.33 sqm
Photographer: Miguel de Guzmán, David Frutos

Amann-Cánovas-Maruri organized the block of flats in accordance with the concept of a simple grouping system based on orderly linear arrangement. The building was designed on top of a previously built reinforced concrete structure. The building allows for individuality of interaction with future users. Inside the space, the furniture is mobile. Versatile hollows on the floor, ceiling, and walls behave as spatial vehicles. The exterior is constructed out of sheet metal, with a ventilated facade and curved corners. The building was envisioned as a set of metallic bodies which left color and finishing choices up to the tenant. There is a range of possibilities to choose from for everything from the color of the facade to the internal layout and finish materials. The project is in this way a strategy for creative housing. The functional system is organized and structured by architects, but final decisions are made by tenants who are building themselves better lives.

EXTERIOR NE

EXTERIOR NO

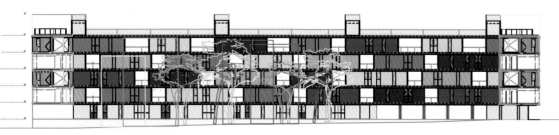

NHOW BERLIN HOTEL
KARIM RASHID

Location: Berlin, Germany
Area: 3,915 sqm
Photographer: Cem Guedes, Patricia Parinejad, Lukas Roth

NHow Berlin hotel celebrates Berlin's modern zeitgeist and connects it to the rest of the world by creating a technorganic land of data-driven art and spaces. Set on the Spree River, the old line between East and West Berlin, the NHow hotel bridges the digital age of information and the physical and spiritual needs of visitors. In NHow, Karim Rashid creates a space that coexists with the digital world. The result is a music inspired hotel where sound is tactile, and a true immersive experience of color, texture, and vibrancy.

"NH Hotels is a large but really smart hotel chain. So when I created the NHow Hotel Berlin my objective was to create an original esoteric place (like Berlin itself) yet one that was still pragmatic and fit into the NH standards. My concept was to engage and fluidity, to speak about music, about diversity, and about eclecticism, but most importantly about the next wave of Berlin. I tried to address all the needs that are intrinsic to living in a simpler and less cluttered, more sensual environment. I always question whether the physical world is as experiential, as seductive, as connective, as inspiring, as personalizable, and as customizable as the digital world. That is what I tried to achieve with NHow Hotel Berlin by making a —space that coexists with the data-driven digital infostethic world." Karim Rashid.

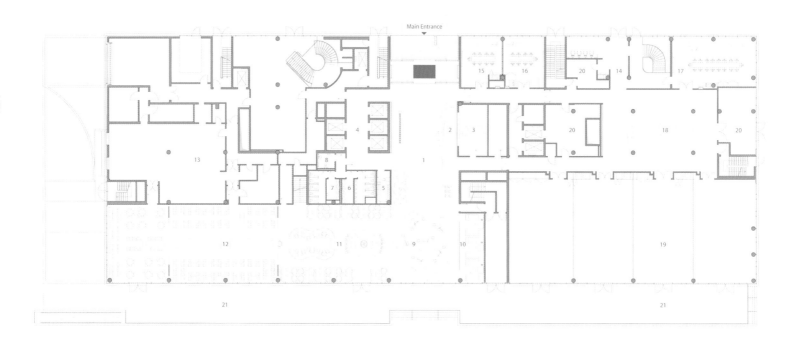

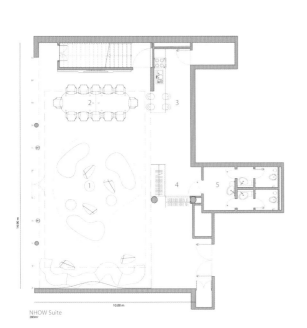

NHOW Suite
280m²

S2 Room
52m²

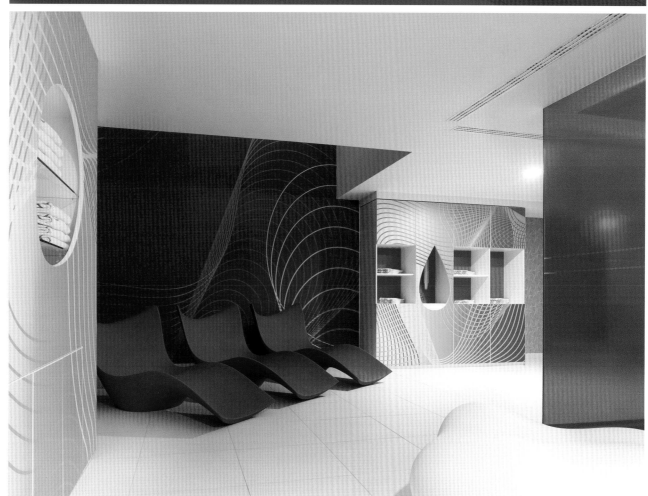

VELEZ-RUBIO NURSERY
ELAP ARQUITECTOS INGENIEROS

Location: Vélez-Rubio, Spain
Area: 874.10 sqm
Photographer: BIS images I Jesus Granada + David Frutos

The building incorporates color in the vinyl laminates of the floors and wall bases. It separates children according to their ages and distinguishes the common spaces from the classrooms. The selection criterion contributes to the development of their psychomotor, mental and social capacities. For the classrooms designed for children under 1 year the color is blue (relaxation, the sea, the world of dreams); classrooms for children between 1 and 2 are painted in orange (psychomotor stimulation, activity); for children between 2 and 3 years of age, the color chosen is green (contact with nature). Common spaces use mixed colors: it is the world of society and the collective.

The program runs easily around a central playground (extension of the dining room or multipurpose room), but the folding of the roof slab deforms the rational stay prism (3.20 m) and wide interior space to the outer limits of the building (5.80 m). On the scale of babies, everything is part of a huge world with an open sky drawn by the nonlinear distribution of the fixtures. The weight of the project rests on the slab and the façade is an element that simply separates the interior from the exterior. But the architects were looking for a connection between this perforation and the user. The circle suggests many analogies (hole, eye, game, moon...) and, above all, it lacks angles and can be used as a table, seat and even as a hammock.

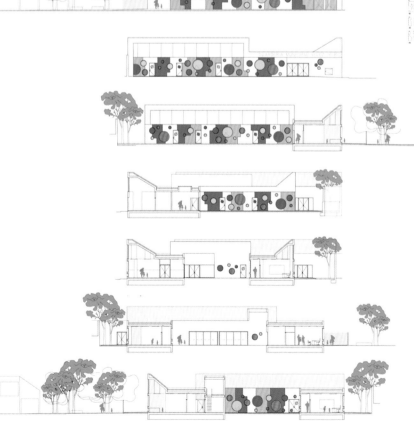

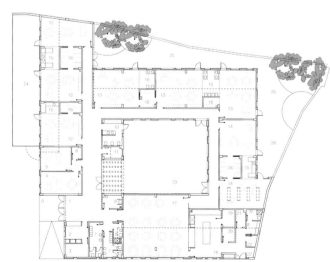

KEKEC KINDERGARTEN
ARHITEKTURA JURE KOTNIK

Location: Ljubljana, Slovenia
Area: 125 sqm
Photographer: Miran Kambič

The main design concept derives from the existing kindergarten's lack of playing equipment. The new façade eliminates this weakness by offering a playing element along all three exterior walls: it consists of dark brown roughcast and timber slats revolving around their vertical axe. The slats are the color of natural wood on one side but are painted in nine different bright colors on the other side. The toy slats offer shade for the windows, as well as provide for children's playing and learning: as the children manipulate the colorful wooden planks they get to know different colors, experience wood as a natural material and constantly change the appearance of their kindergarten, all at the same time. Children rarely get the opportunity to connect with their kindergarten in such a way, to play with it and change the way it looks, as is the case with Kekec.

Playrooms are compact but allow for the furniture to be arranged in various formations. Daylight floods the interior from three sides as well as from the roof. Located between the two playrooms, washrooms have large glass openings, which visually increase their volume as well as ease tutor supervision. Wardrobes in the narrow changing room are made from pure natural wood and have pull-out boxes for shoes in all the colors of the façade, which also serve as a bench, hence functioning as a space saver. Although modest in size, Kekec is a clear example of how a problem solving architecture can supplement and enrich anonymous existing structures within a very limited budget.

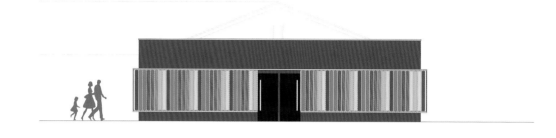

LAMELLAS PALETTE

FACADE RAINBOW

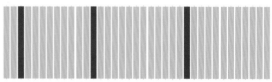

WOOD vs. PANTONE 674 C

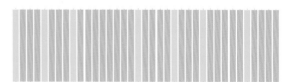

WOOD vs. PANTONE 394 C

ZIGZAG IN TIANJIN
SAKO ARCHITECTS

Location: Tianjin, China
Area: 33,748 sqm
Photographer: Misae HIROMATSU - Ruijing Photo

This is a middle school and primary school project for a large-scale development in Tianjin, China. The first phase of the project contains a primary school and a library. The second phase contains a middle school, a gymnasium and a dining hall. Eight bands of the 4-storey structure for the primary school are created in a Zigzag shape and round shapes are used all over the place to create amusing space. There is a huge roof between schoolhouses and it creates semi-outdoor public space. The semi outdoor public space has sunlight from round skylights on the roof and wind from between schoolhouses. Because of the semi-outdoor environment, the public spaces are used regardless of seasons and weather. Children can run around and play together, or have a performance here. There are 12 bridges to connect the general classroom building and the special classroom building which are located facing each other across the public space, and the scene of children crossing imparts vitality to the space. The elevation becomes patterned indented and varied by using bay window shaped boxes for air-conditioning units.

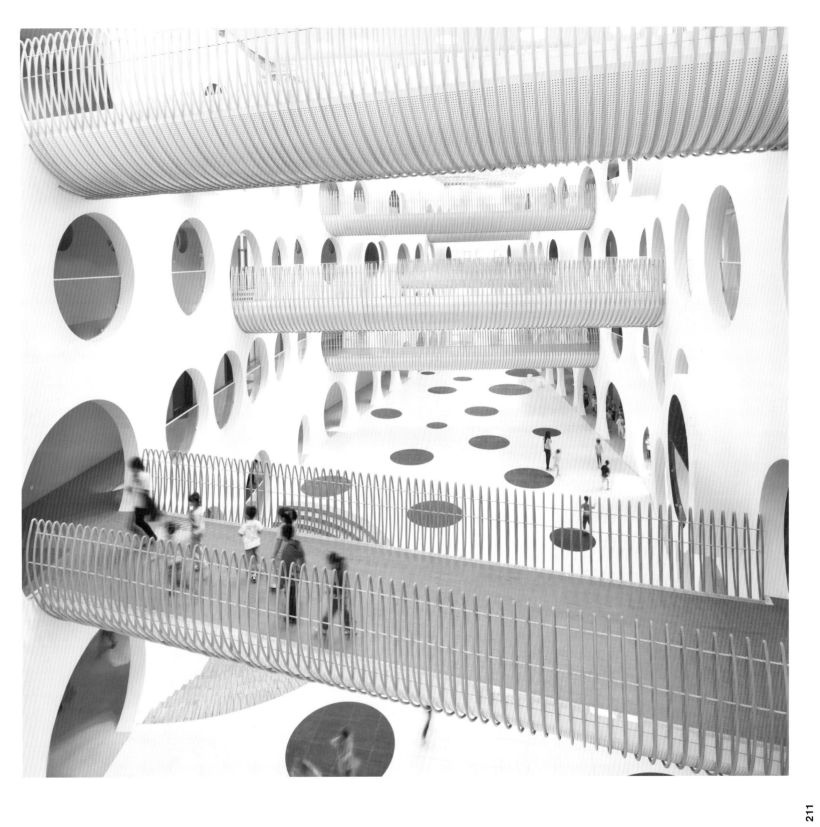

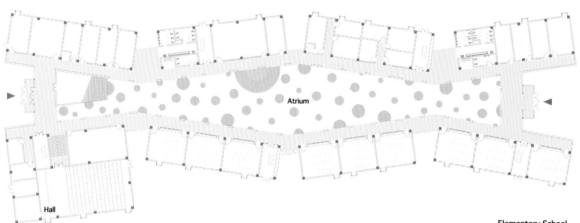

Atrium

Hall

Elementary School
1F Plan

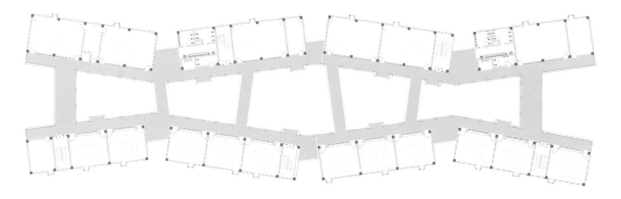

Elementary School
4F Plan

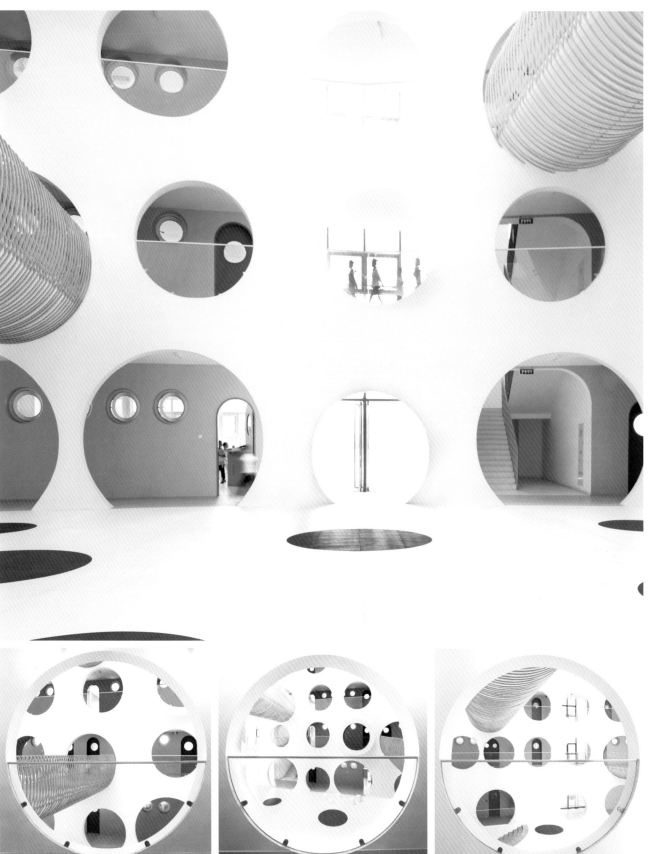

PRISMATIC COLORS
JEAN VERVILLE ARCHITECTE

Location: Montreal, Canada
Area: 140 sqm
Photographer: Jean Verville Architecte

To satisfy a client who wanted his home life to stimulate creativity and lead him to explore new avenues of work, Verville created an environment that distilled the essence of its owner. Using minimal interventions and simple materials, the architect awakens the senses and blurs the perception of the space. Using five colored pencils in the client's favorite shades, Verville sketched on white paper what was to be the background of the project. He designed an open dwelling that would host the client's large collection of artworks and created storage solutions so that the owner can rotate the pieces on display, engaging in a process of constant renewal of the space.

The interventions performed at the architectural level modify the usual domestic proportions and help to offer an extraordinary experience. Whether they are white, colored, or paneled with mirrors, the cabinets structure the space of the loft. They multiply perspectives and add to the overall reflectiveness on the shiny floor to offer a multiplied space. The all-yellow sleeping space also contains concealed storage chests and becomes a multipurpose sculptural space. Throughout, the large, the small, and the tiny rub shoulders, accentuating contrasts of scale. The floor has insertions of colored vinyl and a glossy epoxy coating, and the palette of paint shades is custom formulated and applied with unique blends prepared by an artist. Ultimately, the project is an experiment in housing that presents a fertile mixture of architecture, art, and design.

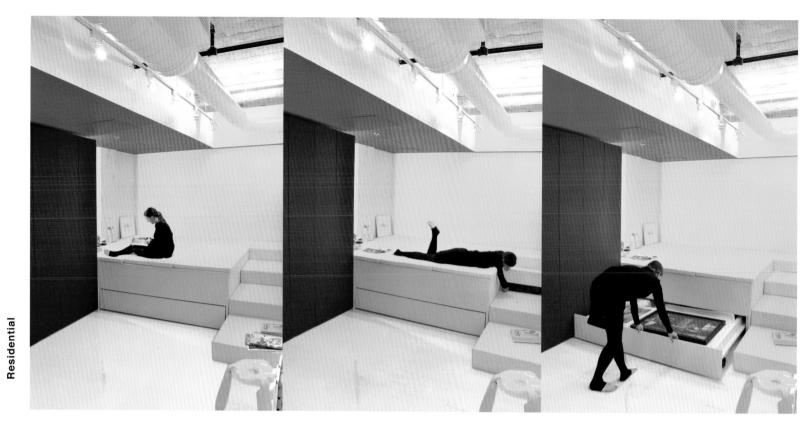

DECAMERON
STUDIO MK27

Location: São Paulo, Brazil
Area: 250 sqm
Photographer: Pedro Vannucchi

The space was constructed through a mixed solution, with maritime transport containers and a specifically designed structure. Despite the spatial limitation imposed by the pre-determined dimension of the containers, the piece has impressive structural attributes that makes stacking them possible. Two stories of containers form tunnels where products are displayed side by side.

The ample span, necessary to show furniture in relation with each other, is formed by a metallic structure. This space is closed in front and in back by double-height metal casements with alveolar polycarbonate. At the back of the lot, there is a patio filled with trees and a pebbled ground. When both doors are simultaneously opened, the whole store becomes integrated with its urban context. At stressful rush hours, by opening only the back doors, the store becomes self-absorbed, ruled by the presence of the inner-garden.

On the back of the site is the office, closed by a glass wall that enables the designers to take part in the sales life. Two edges of the design process make contact in the inner patio as other opposing strengths also meet at this point: the intensity of urban life and the retreat of nature, the power of the containers and the lightness of the metallic structure, and finally, the linear tunnels and the cubic volume.

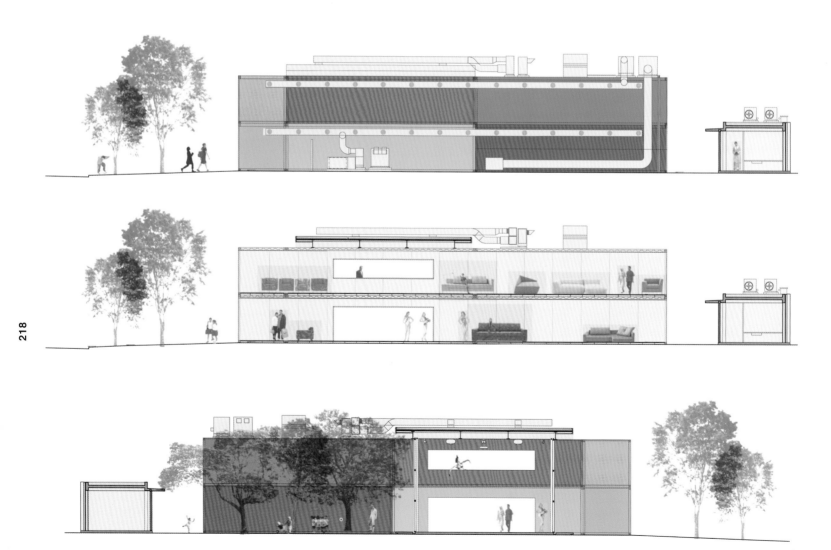

d

FUEL CAFÉ AT CHESAPEAKE
ELLIOTT + ASSOCIATES ARCHITECTS

Location: Oklahoma City, USA
Area: 354.98 sqm
Photographer: Scott McDonald, Hedrich Blessing

Hip and high energy are the key words here. The team started out with a bland, 354.98 sqm are-foot space that used to house Chesapeake's accounting department. It had natural light on three sides, but that was it for visual excitement. The ceilings were low, the floors gray, and the general atmosphere gloomy. The architects gutted it to create a clean, white space, essentially a large reflector, to which they added T8 fluorescents with color gels, LED lamps, and laminated-glass panels with polyester film. There are no computers, fancy fixtures, or any sophisticated dimmers. Yet from this bare-bones technology comes a stunning range of intense color that complements the food being served: banana yellow and chili-pepper red, the cool pink of watermelon, and the deep purple of eggplant. The cooking island in the center of the restaurant is covered in red and green resin panels, like a floating Italian salad.

FUEL celebrates the interplay of color and daylight, with color being a starting point and first principle for the architect instead of a decorative afterthought.

The café has as many moods as the day: soft and welcoming in the morning, bright and upbeat at lunch, subdued in the late afternoon. The light is multidirectional as it streams through laminated-glass panels, bounces off walls and floors, and zips across ceilings in vibrant fluorescent stripes. Even mechanical chases are light sources. The glowing rectangular boxes at opposite ends of the café, with their green and blue LED lights, hide the exhausts from the prep kitchen below. Everywhere colors intersect and overlap, turning the interior into a Fauve painting.

But FUEL is more than a hip design statement; it is part of a strategy to enrich the corporate culture. By providing fresh, healthful, cooked-to-order food, it is a way to boost productivity and promote in-house socializing without making employees feel that they're settling for less.

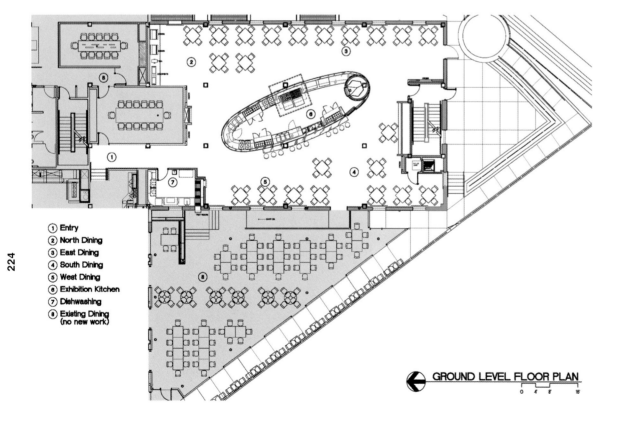

1. Entry
2. North Dining
3. East Dining
4. South Dining
5. West Dining
6. Exhibition Kitchen
7. Dishwashing
8. Existing Dining
   (no new work)

GROUND LEVEL FLOOR PLAN

0   4   8   16'

FEDERAL WAY ELEMENTARY SCHOOLS
ARCHETYPE-PANTHER LAKE
DLR GROUP

Location: Washington, USA
Area: Each school is between 4,088sqm and 5,017sqm
Photographer: Chris J. Roberts

To plan the Archetype on a flexible model, the design team re-examined existing assumptions about educational needs. Initial studies revisited the school's existing program, and found the opportunity to simplify the list of spaces into groupings by type (size, basic function, systems needs). The team then distilled this simplified list into a program of fundamental learning spaces, where each space is defined by capacity and usage patterns. This generic program is a huge change in K-12 design. It supports each school's current, specific program needs but gives them ample ability to adapt to changes over time.

The architectural concept enables adaptation based on site-specific influencing factors, including immediate site topography, surrounding community patterns of use and access, and district-wide relationships. In accordance with the client's goals, the archetype is readily recognizable by its consistent use of an architectural language of lower volumes ("bars") and higher volumes ("lanterns"), and the application of color.

While all spaces engage users through bold color, natural daylight and connections to the outdoors, the geometric formality of the north-south learning spaces contrasts with a playful Network transept. The Network provides a clear connecting pathway (from the western public side of the school to the library/wetlands on the west) for student and community use of the school. Individual areas for different uses (group learning, gathering, events, play, display, library, lunchroom, etc.) are defined by structural accents and color, but remain largely open to one another, encouraging progression and connection through the school while still providing distinct spaces.

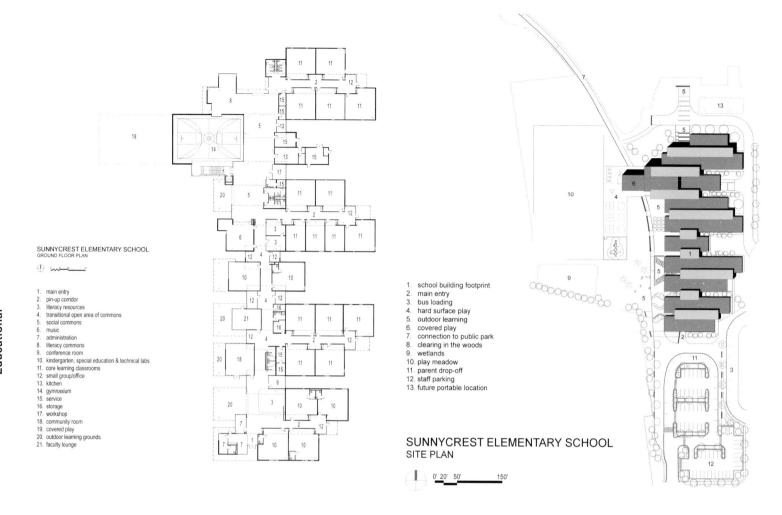

SUNNYCREST ELEMENTARY SCHOOL
GROUND FLOOR PLAN

1. main entry
2. pin-up corridor
3. literacy resources
4. transitional open area of commons
5. social commons
6. music
7. administration
8. literacy commons
9. conference room
10. kindergarten, special education & technical labs
11. core learning classrooms
12. small group/office
13. kitchen
14. gymnasium
15. service
16. storage
17. workshop
18. community room
19. covered play
20. outdoor learning grounds
21. faculty lounge

1. school building footprint
2. main entry
3. bus loading
4. hard surface play
5. outdoor learning
6. covered play
7. connection to public park
8. clearing in the woods
9. wetlands
10. play meadow
11. parent drop-off
12. staff parking
13. future portable location

SUNNYCREST ELEMENTARY SCHOOL
SITE PLAN

0' 20' 50'   150'

Cerejeira Fontes Arquitectos

www.imago.com.pt

Imago is an architectural design and engineering firm located in Braga, Portugal. For 15 years we have provided programming and full design services for various projects. The firm is organized in multiple departments: Architectural, Engineering, Urban planning, Interior design and Project Management. In each of these departments, there are colleagues from the University of Minho collaborating with us. Projects vary from residential, commercial, and institutional to urban planning.

p.090 – 093

Clavel Arquitectos

www.clavel-arquitectos.com

Clavel Arquitectos specialize in singular projects that are technically viable and also meet with economic, social, environmental and administrative requirements. Clients, neighbors, and customers are all closely linked to the design process from the start and their diversity is taken into account in the design and when searching for solutions to the proposed objectives.

Our numerous projects that have been awarded prove that it is possible to offer the best in architectural design and comply with strict budgets and deadlines. In order to do so, we have a strong multidisciplinary team made up of architects, engineers, biologists and interior designers, all of whom are indispensible due to the diverse and complex projects we deal with.

From very large scale to small interior design projects, we select our projects not for their size or budget but for the potential they have to help create.

p.030 – 033

Craig & Karl

www.craigandkarl.com

Craig Redman and Karl Maier live in different parts of the world but collaborate daily to create bold work that is filled with simple messages executed in a thoughtful and often humorous way. They specialize in illustration and installation.

Craig & Karl have exhibited across the world, most notably at the Musée de la Publicité, Louvre. They have worked on projects for clients like LVMH, Google, Nike, Apple, Vogue and The New York Times. Craig is the creator of the blog Darcel Disappoints, often working in collaboration with iconic Parisian store colette.

p.100 –101

Daigo Ishii + Future-scape Architects.

www.future-scape.co.jp

Daigo Ishii was born in Tokyo, Japan in 1960. He graduated from the Department of Architecture, Waseda University with a Bachelors of Engineering and then the Graduate School of Architecture, Waseda University with a Masters of Engineering. He worked for Hiroshi Hara + Atelier and City and Architecture Planning Office since then. In 1999, he established Future-scape Architects. He was a Visiting Lecturer at Waseda University and Japan University of Industy.

p.120-123

De-Spec

www.de-spec.com

De-Spec is a multi-disciplinary international design and 'Think Tank' firm working with a broad range of clients with a specialty in 'retail', 'medi-spa', 'hospitality' and the anchor point of all design 'residential'. Using ideas of 'Radical functionalism' we provide clients with intelligent, innovative and exciting solutions which include research, showing 'trends' and 'future needs' and sensitivity to sustainability. We view design as more than a marketing tool and strive to organize each company's identity and define its built environment which serves to refine the 'brand experience' as a concept. In today's economy we partner to help with creative thinking, strategic planning and analysis to refine the program to evolve into a new and more relevant models for the new economic landscape.

p.010 – 011

DLR Group

www.dlrgroup.com

DLR Group is an interdisciplinary design firm providing architecture, engineering, planning, and interior design from offices coast-to-coast and in China. Our promise is to elevate the human experience through design. This promise inspires sustainable design for a diverse group of public and private sector clients, local communities, and our planet. DLR Group fully supports the initiatives and goals of the 2030 Challenge and is an initial signatory to the AIA 2030 Commitment.

p.182 – 185/p.226 –231

Dominique Coulon & Associés

www.coulon-architecte.fr

Dominique Coulon was born in 1961. In 1989 he graduated with the professor and architect Henri Ciriani and he created his own studio.

Concepts for sustainable development, respect for historical context and responsibility towards the environment and its ecologies are amongst the main concerns for the agency.

As a way to find a new dynamic approach to each architectural project, the agency's methodology draws upon the rich exchange of information stemming from interdisciplinary work. Complexity becomes the catalyst for architectural projects.

Since 2008, Sarah BREBBIA , Olivier Nicollas and Steve Letho Duclos have joined the office as associates, thereby becoming Dominique Coulon et Associés.

p.076 – 081

dosmasuno arquitectos

www.dosmasunoarquitectos.com

Ignacio Borrego (ETSA Madrid 2000), Nestor Montenegro (ETSA Madrid 2002) and Lina Toro (UPB Medellin 2001) formed dosmasuno arquitectos in 2002.

They have been prize winners in more than 30 national and international competitions, among which the following could be highlighted: Social Services Centre in Mostoles, 67 dwellings in

Colmenar Viejo, University Central Library and Museum in Alcala de Henares, Madrid, 102 dwellings for the EMVS in Madrid, 17 dwellings for the EMVS in Madrid, all of them under different phases of construction, together with Europan 7 in Slovenia and Spain, Casa de las Artes in Cadiz, Reorganisation of the Llano Amarillo in Algeciras and the Masterplan for the Campus of Justice in Madrid.

ELAP arquitectos ingenieros

www.elap.es

ELAP is a firm founded by LosdelDesierto / The Desert Ones -Eva Luque + Alejandro Pascual. She is an architect and graphic designer & he is an architect and engineer.

They focus their work on several aspects like creativity, innovation, low cost, sustainability etc. But their primary goals are to dialogue with the environment and especially the link with users. Their work has been internationally and nationally awarded on numerous occasions and published in a long list of international publications of architecture and design.

elips design

www.elipsdesign.com

elips design, a design and research studio based in London, RIBA,is a chartered Practice. Even if the practice remains dedicated to the realization of buildings, it also operates in area beyond the traditional boundaries of architecture, including semiotics, renewable energy, technology, product design and graphic design. It has always been guided by a belief that the quality of our surroundings has a direct influence on the quality of our lives, whether that is in the workplace, at home or in the public realm. Allied to that is an acknowledgement that architecture is generated by the needs of people – both material and spiritual – and a concern for the physical context and the culture and climate of place. Equally, excellence of design and its successful execution are central to our approach. Environmental awareness is an integral part of the practice's culture as it evolves to meet the challenges of the next years.

Elliott + Associates Architects

www.e-a-a.com

Established in 1976, Elliott + Associates Architects is a full-service architectural firm of licensed architects, interior and graphic designers and support personnel. The firm has designed award-winning projects for corporate clients, various arts organizations, museums, and public spaces.

The design philosophy of the firm is shaped from the theory that a space reflects the unique personality of the owner, coupled with functionality. Elliott + Associates Architects creates special environments - architectural portraits - revealed as expressions of the client. The goal is to examine together who the client is, where he is going, and what he wants to accomplish. Defining the essence of who he is and his objectives enables the development of concepts to address the issues that forn the basis of the portrait.

emmanuelle moureaux

www.emmanuelle.jp

French architect and designer residing in Tokyo since 1996. She established "emmanuelle moureaux architecture + design" in 2003. Inspired by the Japanese traditional sliding screens, Emmanuelle has created the concept of "Shikiri", which literally means "dividing (creating) space with colors" in English. She uses colors as three-dimensional elements, like layers, in order to create spaces, and not as a finishing touch applied on surfaces. Architecture, interior, furniture and products - she designs a wide range of projects, by using her unique technique of color scheming and handling colors as space makers. Associate professor at the Tohoku University of Art & Design. Member of the "Tokyo society of architects".

FUJIMURA DESIGN STUDIO

fujimura-ds.com

MASUO FUJIMURA was born in Gifu, Japan in 1964. He worked under TOGASHI DESIGN STUDIO until 1998 and established FUJIMURA DESIGN STUDIO in 1999. He has designed a wide range of projects including WEDGWOOD SHOP, LE CEUSET SHOP, Korean Barbeque Restaurant 'An-Kissho', Bansho-ji Temple Ossuary Crystal Palace, Bridal Jewelry Shop 'LUZIR' etc. With a design philosophy of "Throughout the design, I hope that you enjoy a better life", his projects were awarded BEST STORE OF THE YEAR in 2008 and 2009.

Geoff Tsui

geofftsui.com

With over 18 years experience as a multidisciplinary designer, creative director/producer, Geoff Tsui has worked alongside international celebrities such as Michelle Yeoh and Jackie Chan. With over 50 movie titles & CD/DVD creative & marketing directions, Geoff has also designed/directed for brands such as Porsche, Maserati, TVB, StarTV, and Jackie Chan Design. His additional architectural & product design background led to numerous bars, shops, events, and residential design projects. Raised in Canada, Geoff adds his cultural background into his multifaceted design talent with a keen sense of business and marketing, serving him currently as co-founder of 33WILL and KONZEPP with Willie Chan.

Golucci International Design

www.golucci.com

Golucci International Design was established by Taiwanese Designer Lee Hsuheng in 2004. Our highly motivated and qualified designers fully recognize the importance of professional acumen. Each project is conceptualized and developed by an experienced design team. Over the years, our works have included a wide range of Clubhouses, Hotels, Bars & Restaurants .

Our management approach ensures high quality for the end effort. We express the essence of our creative ideas in ways that best benefit our clients.

HAMONIC + MASSON

www.hamonic-masson.com

Founded in 1997 by Gaëlle Hamonic (born 1968) and Jean-Christophe Masson (1967), and winner of the 2002 "Nouveaux Albums de la Jeune Architecture" award, the agency made its mark in 2003 by designing one of two prototypes (the "Maison en Styltech") for a contemporary home exhibited in the Parc de la Villette in Paris.

The agency sets itself apart by its fusion of rigorous construction, practical design, the use of original materials, and its thinking about urban typologies. It has been awarded numerous housing development projects in densely populated areas (particularly in Paris), as well as cultural facilities (Records Office) and school and tertiary programs. All fifteen completed projects are radical and contemporary in character.

Jean de Lessard

www.delessard.com

An International designer based in Montreal, Jean de Lessard, with more than 20 years experience, has designed numerous interiors, particularly in the commercial and deluxe residential sectors. His eclectic skill set has led him to work on spaces with very diverse uess - from corporate offices to hotels and interiors of restaurants and boutiques.

In 2010, de Lessard received the prestigious International Best Interior Design Americas award in London, UK. He has also won the Prix Intérieurs | Ferdie competition, and awards from the Institut Design Montréal. He is a member of the Club des Ambassadeurs des Grands Prix du Design.

Jean Verville Architecte

www.jeanverville.com

Jean Verville's architectural practice is based on experimentation and exploration. In each of his projects – residential or commercial, installation or scenography – he imagines architecture as akin to sculpture. He transposes lines and volumes in an almost immaterial reality, projecting the user into the sketch. His structures present sculptural volumes with a strong materiality that amplifies their expressiveness. His attention fully focuses on unique architecture using simple means.

This year, Verville opened up his practice with a collaboration with singer-songwriter Pierre Lapointe. Together, they created a remarkable installation for the Big Bang exhibition at the Montreal Museum of Fine Art. Currently, in addition to designing three residences, he is planning a research trip to Japan, where he will develop an experiential residential concept.

JGMA

www.jgma.co

JGMA is a progressive architecture and design practice committed to interdisciplinary collaboration, active community involvement and the enrichment of peoples' lives through attentive and dynamic organization of space and materiality. We understand that architecture and design has a unique ability to influence civic life and transform communities.

Based in Chicago, we have successfully executed design projects at all scales from small to extra-large in North America, Latin America, Asia and the Middle East. Our team represents a diverse collaboration of experienced architectural professionals with a vast portfolio of public and private work in the areas of education, research and technology, hospitality, residential, healthcare, commercial, interiors, urban and master planning, product design and graphic design.

JULIO BARRENO ARCHITECT

www.juliobarreno.com

Julio Barreno Gutiérrez: Graduated from the School of Architecture of Seville in 1996. Associate Professor at School of Architecture of Seville since 2001.

ARCHITECT-PROFESSOR invited by different organizations as Junta de Andalucía, the international University of Andalucía in Baeza, the School of architecture of Granada, the school of architecture of the Royal Danish Academy of Fine Arts of Copenhagen, Texas Tech University School of Architecture, the architect's association of Cadiz, the Facultade de Arquitectura da Universidade do Porto and the Department of architecture of Cambridge (U.K.), to participate in several lectures. He has been published in different kinds of competitions of architecture or workshops of architecture; with publications in several specialized magazines such as Neutra, Arquitectura Viva, Pasajes de Arquitectura Contemporánea, Culturas, and also in several catalogues of expositions. Selected architect for the Spanish Young Architects Exposition organized by the Housing Ministry that start on October 2007.

Karim Rashid

karimrashid.com

Karim Rashid is one of the most prolific designers of his generation. Over 3000 designs in production, over 300 awards and works in over 40 countries attest to Karim's legend of design.

His award winning designs include luxury goods for Christofle, Veuve Clicquot, and Alessi, democratic products for Umbra, Bobble, and 3M, furniture for Bonaldo and Vondom, lighting for Artemide and Fabbian, high tech products for Asus and Samsung, surface design for Marburg and Abet Laminati, brand identity for Citibank and Sony Ericsson and packaging for Method, Paris Baguette, Kenzo and Hugo Boss.

Klein Dytham architecture

klein-dytham.com

Klein Dytham architecture (KDa) is a multi-disciplinary design practice known for architecture, interiors, public spaces and installations. Established by Royal College of Art graduates Mark Dytham and Astrid Klein in Tokyo in 1991, today KDa is a multi-lingual office with a rising international reputation and an increasingly high-profile client list.

KDa's built work includes flagship retail stores, restaurants, resort facilities, office fitouts, houses and apartments. KDa has no stylistic recipe, preferring to work with the client, program and other project parameters to develop a uniquely tailored solution. Materials, technology, and context are all key elements of KDa's design approach, spiced always with an irreverent or surprising twist.

p.160 – 163

Kois Associated Architects

koisarchitecture.com

Kois Associated Architects is based in Athens and was founded by architect Stelios Kois in 2007. K.A.A's work encompasses all fields of design, ranging from urban projects to private buildings, interiors, furniture and products. The design ethos of the collaboration is the synchronized engagement in practice and research that leads to the evaluation and generation of new solutions. Research topics are drawn from natural forms and the social sciences in an attempt to form an interdisciplinary network of information that will inform the decision making process. We work in a continuous workshop spirit with a multidisciplinary team of architects, engineers, graphic artists and town planners from very different cultural backgrounds. The practice's view is that only through diversity and antithesis can true innovative solutions emerge and manifest themselves.

p.166 – 169

kräf•te, Yukio Kimura

mdnc-krafte.com

kräf•te is an Osaka-based Interior Design firm. We are able to provide total design solutions from VI development to Graphic design and Product design that goes along with the Interior Design. With our portfolio category we not only aim to exhibit, but also to propose a means of expressing works in order to pursue a uniqueness only available at our gallery.

p.082 – 085

LIM TAE HEE design studio

www.limtaeheestudio.com

Taehee Lim majored in Interior architecture in Korea. She then attended Kyoto Institute of Technology where she received her ph.D in architecture.

She is currently running "LIM TAE HEE design studio" which she founded in 2007 shortly after her return to Korea.

LIM TAE HEE design studio covers a wide range of design including residential, office and commercial areas and has been involved in many design exhibitions.

She is continuing her career in teaching design as well as writing about design, culture and architecture.

p.068 – 071

Manuelle Gautrand Architecture

www.manuelle-gautrand.com

Manuelle Gautrand is the principal architect and director of the Parisian agency Manuelle Gautrand Architecture. She mainly designs buildings in areas as diverse as cultural facilities (theaters, museums, and cultural centers), office buildings, housing, commercial and leisure facilities, etc…

Among her leading projects in recent years are the "C42" Citroen Flagship Showroom on the Champs Elysees Avenue in Paris for which she gained attention and widespread acclaim in the international arena and from a large audience, the Gaité Lyrique, a conversion of a historical theatre into a center for contemporary and digital arts and music in Paris, and the "LaM" - Lille Museum of Modern, Contemporary and Outsider art.

p.050 – 053

MARKETING-JAZZ

www.marketing-jazz.com

MARKETING-JAZZ is the #1/leading company in Spain specialized in visual marketing. Founded by Carlos Aires in 2002, MARKETING-JAZZ focuses on creating new store concepts to improve sales. Its retail projects include creative and integral store designs, branding and communication through window displays and training and providing specialized expertise in visual merchandising.

p.064 – 067

McBride Charles Ryan

www.mcbridecharlesryan.com.au/

At MCR, we have one passion——providing exceptional design for our clients.

Our commitment to provide our clients with innovative solutions, technical excellence and personal and professional integrity has generated a steady growth in the reputation of our company since 1988.

MCR has successfully managed projects with budgets of up to $200M, combining complex architectural forms with the finest construction techniques and the most demanding programs. We have experience in many areas, having undertaken and realized work in all sectors, and this has been recognized by a variety of awards. In 2005, we were awarded the highest Victorian award, the Victorian Architecture Medal. In 2009 we received the World Architecture Festival award for the 'Best House' Category.

McBride Charles Ryan prides itself in its hands-on approach to its projects and believe that our buildings are bespoke manifestations of our clients' vision and it is due to this approach that our designs are truly singular. We never arrive at a problem already knowing the answer.

p.152 – 155

Mi5 architects

www.mi5arquitectos.com

Mi5 is the team of Manuel Collado and Nacho Martin which since 1999 has focused on researching unexplored architecture project strategies. Our works have been recognized, awarded and published on several occasions.

We have been invited to VII Venice Architecture Biennale, Europe VI Burgos, Liege and MOPU, COAM Recent Work Foundation, FRESHMADRID COAM Foundation, Madrid Social Housing RIBA (London), 100% Crude COAM Foundation, Building Dwelling Thinking IVAM, etc.

We have taught at the Architectural Association in London, Architectural Polytechnic Universities of Alicante (UA), Alcala de Henares (UAH) and Camilo Jose Cela in Madrid, and Fashion Design at the European Institute of Design (IED Madrid) , in addition to having participated in several workshops, juries and lectures.

Ministry of Design

www.modonline.com

Ministry of Design was created by Colin Seah to Question, Disturb & Redefine the spaces, forms and experiences that surround us and give meaning to our world. An integrated experiential-design practice, MOD's explorations are created amidst a democratic 'studio-like' atmosphere and progress seamlessly between form, site, object and space. We love to question where the inherent potential in contemporary design lies, and then to disturb the ways projects are created or perceived – redefining the world around us in relevant and innovative ways, one project at a time!

Palatre et Leclere Architectes

www.palatreleclere.com

The Palatre et Leclere Architectes agency arose from the meeting between Tiphaine Leclere and Olivier Palatre, connected to a wish of development and sharing. Many international publications have profiled the success of the agency.

"The peculiarity of our architecture lies in its sensitivity and in the forms, subjects and colors articulated.

The aesthetic feeds on technicality and on the formal research.

The projects, more and more sensory, vibrate in relation with a musical universe.

We chose architecture as a field of intervention to intervene in the scale of the domestic space in the city."

Pedra Silva Architects

www.pedrasilva.com

Pedra Silva Architects is an architectural design office based in Brighton and Lisbon that caters to for all aspects of architectural and interior design. Our work ranges from small-scale projects with an emphasis in leading retail brands to large scale multi-million investments.

In retail we develop architectural designs associated with pioneering concepts for restaurants, retail spaces, health care centers and office spaces. We currently work with a portfolio of international clients that are key players in these sectors.

On larger scale projects, we develop all phases of project design including project management. Besides architectural services our offices provide a hub that bridges cultural gaps for foreign investment in local economies.

The majority of work is currently in Europe with an expansion moving towards emerging markets in Africa, Middle East and Asia.

Périphériques architectes

www.peripheriques-architectes.com

For 15 years, Périphériques architectes has been a scalable structure that explores the production and distribution of architecture and urban planning. Currently composed of 2 agencies Marin + Trottin architects and Anne - Françoise twin architects / afja, Périphériques architectes offer a creation, based on negotiation and the sharing of ideas as well as multidisciplinary activities.

Périphériques architectes operates mainly in the fields of architecture and urban planning. Our experience focuses on housing, cultural facilities, as well as educational space.

PS Arkitektur

www.psarkitektur.com

We enhance our clients' image and business capacity through innovative architecture and design. Our motto is "architecture for change."

We work with a broad range of projects ranging from urban planning to buildings and commercial interiors. Our aim is to create unique buildings and interiors that speak for themselves.

We reveal the potential, visualize the hidden and suggest improvements. Architecture and design is a means of competition that creates value. In cooperation with the client we define the specifications and goals of the project in order to create a design that communicates and strengthens the client's identity.

Rearquitectura

www.rearquitectura.cl

Rearquitectura was founded in 2004 by two young architects, Cristian Barrientos and Antonio Menéndez. Rearquitectura's expertise is in collective housing, hotels and commercial buildings. The design philosophy is to develop projects with unique architecture that respects the urban surroundings without compromising the contemporary design of the building. Apart from designing architecture projects for external clients, Rearquitectura also designs and develops its own real estate housing buildings. This is the case of Lofts Yungay II, in which all the stages of the project were managed by Rearquitectura.

ROW Studio

rowarch.com

ROW Studio is an architecture and design firm directed by Álvaro Hernández Felix, Nadia Hernández Felix and Alfonso Maldonado Ochoa since 2005. Its name derives from the term used in economy to refer to global phenomena (ROW: Rest of the World), as a critical standpoint against the clichés of Mexican architecture and the need to generate an international discourse both in processes and proposals departing from a multidisciplinary approach. At the same time the studio addresses the need to expand field studies and architectural methods from architecture to other disciplines such as sociology, psychology, economy, marketing, etc.

SAKO Architects

www.sako.co.jp

SAKO Architects offers a wide range of design related services, ranging from architectural and interior design to graphical, sign, furniture, landscape design and urban planning.

We are experienced in residential and commercial designs, and have also dealt with design types like government buildings and museums.

Our interior design works have been awarded with Jury's Best Award and Honorable Mentions in JCD Design Award, successively over the last seven years and our architectural design works have been awarded with a large number of prizes in China.

SAVVY STUDIO

savvy-studio.net

We are a multi-disciplinary studio dedicated to developing brand experiences that generate emotional links between our clients and their audience.

Our team is composed of specialists in the areas of marketing, communication, graphic design, industrial design, creative copywriting and architecture. We also collaborate with talented artists and designers from around the world, a process that allows us to offer creative and innovative solutions with a global competitive edge.

We approach every project with a comprehensive and open creative process, which facilitates the participation of our clients in every step.

Sergey Makhno

www.mahno.com.ua

Sergey Makhno is an artist, architect, designer, and workshop project manager. In 1999 he founded "Makhno workshop". Sergey believes that his imaginative vision is the combination of contradictory backgrounds and creation of artistic mixes from seemingly incompatible things. He never rests, instead spending his free time visiting international design exhibitions and antique shops.

He invents things, sometimes reinventing forgotten objects but often creating new objects never thought of before. Apart from interiors, he designs original furniture, produces pictures, collages, and collects antique suitcases, eau-fortes, towels, radio-phonographs, and scissors.

SOMOS.ARQUITECTOS

www.somosarquitectos.es

SOMOS.ARQUITECTOS arises like an open-minded association which merges ideas, images and concepts which serve as a base to construct a collection of realities that allow a free approach to the contemporary urban landscape. We provide specific solutions to specific problems whether we are working on interior design, building, teaching or researching. We do not believe so much in "styles" as in the sensible experience of contemporary reality. The expressive richness of each and every one of the associates composing the studio is a powerful tool to re-initiate, re-pose, re-think and re-activate the creative process. We rely highly on public competitions, but Education as well as Research activities are additional areas of interaction which in the end are necessary to enrich our architectural based firm.

studio mk27

www.studiomk27.com.br

studio mk27 was founded at the beginning of the 1980s by Marcio Kogan, an architect who graduated from Mackenzie University in 1976, and today is made up of more than 20 architects, as well as collaborators located in various parts of the world. The architects of the studio develop the projects from start to finish, and co-sign their authorship. Recently, the office has won several international awards, such as: Record House, in 2004 and 2005, the D&AD "Yellow Pencil" in 2008 and 2009, the Dedalo Minosse in 2008 and the Barbara Cappochin of the Padova International Biennial in 2007, besides important Brazilian ones, such as 12 awards from the IAB and the recent: Wallpaper Design Awards in 2010 and The World Architecture Festival – WAF in 2011. The architectural projects of studio mk27 highly prioritize formal simplicity, always taking great care with details and finishing. Marcio Kogan and the team, great admirers of the Brazilian modernist generation, strive to undertake the difficult mission of giving continuity to this line of production.

Studio Ramin Visch

www.raminvisch.com

Studio Ramin Visch was established in 1998 and is a professional team with an office in Amsterdam.

Field of activity – Our projects are best described as large scale interior projects. Projects vary from a cinema to an espresso bar, apartments, furniture, offices and exhibitions. From interior and renovation to architecture,a Large part of our projects is realized in industrial heritage or industrial monuments.

Design aproach – The old and new are clearly kept separate, both in materialization and volume. This clear distinction between new and old enhances both. Although the function of the building changes, its spaciousness and character are preserved and remain omnipresent throughout the building. Together with a team of architects, constructors, acoustics professionals and light experts we are involved in all phases of the process, from design to delivery.

Quality – Lucidity, tranquility and spaciousness. Creation of the interior as clear intimacy of space.

Studio Up

www.studioup.hr

Lea Pelivan and Toma Plejic established STUDIO UP at the end of 2003. The Zagreb-based firm concerns itself with contemporary architecture and urbanism. They received the Grand Prix of the 2003 Zagreb Salon and represented Croatia at the 2004 Venice Biennale, 9th International Exhibition of Architecture, and participated at the "Mare Nostrum" exhibition and Power Lounge as a part of the 2nd and 3rd International Rotterdam Biennale of Architecture. In 2008 they were part of the exhibitions "Balkanology" in Basel, "Peacebuilding" in Rome and "New trajectories: Contemporary Architecture in Croatia and Slovenia" in Boston.

TORAFU ARCHITECTS

torafu.com

Founded in 2004 by Koichi Suzuno and Shinya Kamuro, TORAFU ARCHITECTS employs a working approach based on architectural thinking. Works by the duo include a diverse range of products, from architectural design to interior design for shops, exhibition space design, product design, spatial installations and film making. Amongst some of their main works are 'TEMPLATE IN CLASKA', 'NIKE 1LOVE', 'BOOLEAN', 'HOUSE IN KOHOKU' and 'airvase' . 'Light Loom (Canon Milano Salone 2011)' was awarded the Grand Prize of the Elita Design Award. Published in 2011 were the 'airvase book' and 'TORAFU ARCHITECTS 2004-2011 Idea + Process' (by BIJUTSU SHUPPAN-SHA CO., LTD.) and in 2012, a picture book titled 'TORAFU's Small City Planning' (by Heibonsha Limited).

Vitruvious & Sons

www.vitruviosons.com

The architectural studio "Vitruvious & Sons" was created by students of the St. Petersburg Academy of Fine Arts in 1994.

Among the first works of the "Vitruvious & Sons" group were project exhibitions and participation in several architectural student competitions.

The "Vitruvious & Sons" architectural studio introduced its first professional projects in 1996.

Witblad

www.witblad.com

Witblad specializes in designing for commercial communication needs. The company offers a full retail package, from corporate identity to interior and website design.

For more than a decade Bob Bulcaen has worked as an interior-architect and internet-architect. In both disciplines the end user and the commercial objectives are the key ingredients to create refreshing and successful designs.

By creating the company Witblad we succeeded in combining these themes into a full retail package to cover all design needs for current companies. Whether it's a new architectural concept, a graphic identity or a new internet strategy, Witblad's strength is the combination of all those fields into one approach. Technological innovations are combined with new design concepts to deliver the best contemporary retail concepts.

Witblad mainly works in the concept, consultancy and design phase of a project.

Z-A Studio

www.z-astudio.com

Z-A is a New York based studio for Architectural Innovation, which is dedicated to exposing the unexpected in the mundane.

Z-A explores Adaptive Materials, Structures and Infrastructures that can adjust and respond to changing needs, uses, users and identities of a project.

Z-A believes that a sustainable project is first and foremost a project that can live longer. A flexible design approach equips the project with the ability to stay relevant over time.

Z-A's designs are a deliberate move away from stylistic or formal uniformity, expressing a genuine interest in the mundane, the found or given condition, which is clearly different from one project to the other. Moreover it is meant to display that starting with the obvious does not have to lead to an obvious result.

ACKNOWLEDGEMENTS

We would like to give our special thanks to all the designers and architects for their kind permission to publish their works, and all the photographers who have generously granted us the right to use their images. Our thanks also go to the assistants, PR people and writers whose names do not appear in the credits. Without your support and assistance, we would not be able to share these amazing colorful spatial design works with readers around the world. Our editorial team includes editor Sasha Lo and book designer Kantrina Leung, to whom we are truly grateful.